# NAVIGATING THE DISTANCES

ALSO BY BRUCE BENNETT

STRAW INTO GOLD

I NEVER DANCED WITH MARY BETH

TAKING OFF *(an Orchises Book)*

# Navigating

## the Distances

*Poems New and Selected*

### Bruce Bennett

ORCHISES

*Washington*

Library of Congress Cataloging in Publication Data

Bennett, Bruce. 1940-
    Navigating the distances : poems new and selected / Bruce Bennett.
        p.   cm.
    ISBN 0-914061-79-8 (alk. paper)
    I. Title.
    PS3532.E54567N3    1998
    811'.54—de 21                          98-50133
                                               CIP

ACKNOWLEDGEMENTS

Poems have been selected from the following books and chapbooks:

Chapbooks: *Coyote Pays A Call*, Bits Press, 1980
            *The Strange Animal*, State Street Press, 1981
            *Not Wanting To Write Like Everyone Else*, State Street Press, 1987
            *To Be A Heron*, FootHills Press, 1989
            *The Garden & Other Abridged Versions*, Bellflower Press, 1990
            *Bare Bones*, Robert L. Barth, 1995
            *It's Hard To Get The Angle Right*, GreenTower Press, 1997
            *Forays*, Clandestine Press, 1998
            *Maneuvers*, Clandestine Press, 1998
            *Garretman*, FootHills Press, 1999

Books:      *Straw Into Gold*, Cleveland State University Press, 1984
            *I Never Danced With Mary Beth*, FootHills Press, 1991
            *Taking Off*, Orchises Press, 1992


Individual poems have been published in the following periodicals, anthologies, and textbooks: *A Coyote Reader* (UNIVERSITY OF CALIFORNIA PRESS), *Ardis Anthology of New American Poetry*, *Bits*, *Bitterroot*, *Brockport Review*, *Clockwatch Review*, *Coyote's Journal*, *The Epigrammatist*, *5 AM*, *The Formalist*, *Harvard Review*, *Hellas*, *Hiram Poetry Review*, *Introduction to Poetry* (LONGMAN), *The Laurel Review*, *Leaving the Bough: 48 Younger American Poets* (INTERNATIONAL PUBLISHERS), *Light*, *Light Year '84*, *Light Year '85*, *Light Year '87*, *Light Year '88/'89*, *Mosaic*, *Piedmont Literary Review*, *Ploughshares*, *Poetry NOW*, *Poets On:*, *Poetry Works!* (MODERN CURRICULUM PRESS), *Poultry*, *Prairie Schooner*, *The Quarterly*, *River Styx*, *St. Andrews Review*, *Seneca Review*, *Sparrow*, *State Street Reader*, *Stet*, *Strong Measures*, *Tar River Poetry*, *Visions*, *Writing Poems* (HARPER/COLLINS).

*Manufactured in the United States of America*

Orchises Press
P. O. Box 20602
Alexandria
Virginia
22320-1602

G6E4C2

The occasion of a *New and Selected Poems* affords the opportunity to discover where one has been, if not where one is going. Also, who and what one has been. The shop has been open for a long time, and all manner of curious objects have issued from it. The reader is invited to browse and inspect, then appropriate and carry away what has been determined to be of value. In the words of "Common Property," the poet borrows and gives back again; "as in a chain," we "pass it on."

This book is dedicated to all those who have passed it on to me.

BRUCE BENNETT

# CONTENTS

IT'S HARD TO GET
THE ANGLE RIGHT

IV.  TAKING OFF

## V.  FLYING HIGH: NEW POEMS

*"a seeker, not a finder yet."*

Herman Melville, "Hawthorne and His Mosses"

*"A man goes far to find out what he is——"*

Theodore Roethke, "In A Dark Time"

*"A man sets himself the task of portraying the world.*
*Through the years he peoples a space with images of provinces,*
*kingdoms, mountains, bays, ships, islands, fishes, rooms,*
*instruments, stars, horses, and people. Shortly before his death,*
*he discovers that that patient labyrinth of lines traces the*
*image of his face."*

Jorge Luis Borges, "Epilogue"

*"It seems to me that I have found what I wanted. When I try to put*
*all into a phrase I say 'Man can embody truth but he cannot know it.'"*

William Butler Yeats, from a last letter

# CALLIGRAPHY

*Ad Majorem Gloriam*

He peered with pleasure at the tiny sign,
a skill it took him all those years to learn.
Noted its graceful curve, the way the line
wavered, but then grew strong at its return.
He wondered whether he too would grow strong
and finish with a flourish, work well done,
God's good and faithful servant. What went wrong?
Why couldn't he simply labor with the sun,
the way he once did, then call it a day?
Why was he subject now to stabs of doubt,
unanswerable questions? Who could say?
He scrutinized his work again. Without
it, nothing mattered; that alone he knew.
Through it he lived, whatever else was true.

# I. THE STORYTELLER

# THE STORYTELLER

They were with him from the beginning: *The Lost Cloud, The Lonely Caterpillar, Voice From The River....* His alone, to be guarded, and hoarded.

Then, he told one. And faces gathered: beautiful faces. He'd never seen such faces. He told more. And more.

He stepped out of the shadows, into a place of light. There was music; laughter. Someone offered her arm. They whirled.

He forgot words... voices....

When, at last, he returned, it was like waking. Or like finding, and trying on, a miraculous coat.

He began telling new ones: *The Man Who Bartered His Name; The Fever; The Old Coat....*

# COYOTE

## COYOTE PAYS A CALL

He came one day
and stayed for a week.

He ate up our food
and asked for more.

He asked to borrow the car—
I told him no.

He began looking at my wife.

I gave him money
but he didn't leave.

"It's nice here," he said.
"I think I'll stay till spring."

I decided to trick him.

I invited Carla
from down the road.

(Carla is large
and very very lonely.)

I told him Carla
had fallen in love.

I had her wait on him.
She whispered in his ear.

That afternoon he was gone.

He took a few things—
a clock, my razor—
but it was worth it.

Don't tell me about Coyote.


## COYOTE RETURNS

One day in winter
I spotted his tracks.

They came around the house
and stopped at the cellar;

then they went on.

"What'd he want in there?"

I checked my toolbox.
Nothing was missing.

Wood was in order.
Wine wasn't touched.

"Funny," I thought.
"He wouldn't come for nothing."

I went upstairs.
"He's been here," I said.

My wife ran to see....
"He's shut off the furnace."

"Son-of-a-bitch!" I shouted.
"I thought it was cold!

Well, get the extra blankets."
It was starting to get dark.

She looked at me funny.

"He took all the blankets.
He said he was freezing.

It's just for the night."


## COYOTE IN DISGUISE

Another time
he came as a beggar.

"I'm down on my luck, Mate.
I need a break."

I offered him food
but he shook his head.

Well, there was this pile
just taking up space:

a sweater, a coat
some shoes, an old hat.

His eyes grew bright.

"I'll not forget you, friend.
You can be sure."

It was just like Christmas:
I got to feel good

and got rid of those clothes....

Well, later that week
I began to get calls.

*"Hey, what's the idea
of takin' my tractor?"*

*"You owe me fifty..."*

*"My daughter confessed..."*

He was using my clothes,
so why not my name?


COYOTE AND THE GYPSIES

A troop of gypsies
camped out of town.

Someone who saw them
raced with the news.

The town went wild—

boats hauled up;
back doors bolted;

children walloped;
shades drawn down.

Everyone braced.

Signs disappeared;
gardens were trampled;

phones went dead;
there were nails in the road...

"Goddam them gypsies!"
somebody hollered.

"Let's get 'em!"

Well, you guessed the rest.
Not a trace of gypsies.

Not a scrap
to show they'd been there.

So somebody asked
"Hey, who was it saw 'em?"

and nobody knew.


## FIND YOUR WAY HOME

Coyote led his son
deep into the forest.

He twirled him around.

"Now, find your way home."

Coyote went home.

"You're alone,"
said his wife.

Coyote laughed.

"He'll be home by supper."

She looked at him hard.

"And what if he isn't?"

Coyote laughed again.

"Then he isn't my son."

## COYOTE TALKS TO BIRDS AND INSTRUCTS HIS SON

Coyote taught his son all of his tricks;
all, except one.

"If I taught you that," Coyote laughed,
"you'd be Coyote."

But Coyote's son was smart.
He wasn't Coyote's son for nothing.
He wanted to learn that trick.

So, one day, he followed
his father into the forest.

When he heard him stop,
he hid under a bush.

Then he peeped out, and listened.

Coyote was talking to birds!

He'd say something, and a bird would swoop
down, perch on his shoulder, fly away, and come
back with a berry or nut, which Coyote would
gobble. Then another would come.

Coyote's son crept closer.
He wanted to learn how his father
talked to birds.

Snap!

Coyote's son howled.

He was hanging, upside down, from a tree!

Coyote strolled over, laughing and laughing.

"That's sure a funny way of walking
through woods, boy."

"I wanted to hear how you talked
to the birds."

"Shucks," chuckled Coyote, cutting him down.
"Any damn fool can talk to birds."


## COYOTE'S METAPHYSICS

"He's bigger than me
and a whole lot smarter,"

Coyote remarked
speaking of God.

"Only thing is
He isn't around much

and it's gotta be someone
lookin' out for the chickens...."

# COYOTE IN NEED

"A name is breath
and breath is wind

and wind is cold
and cold needs fire,"

chattered the stranger
warming his hands.

"I'll give you a name
if it's names you're after.

You can take your pick
on a night like this."

# STRAW INTO GOLD

## THE TRUE STORY OF SNOW WHITE

Almost before the Princess had grown cold
Upon the floor beside the bitten fruit,
The Queen gave orders to her men to shoot
The dwarfs, and thereby clinched her iron hold
Upon the state. Her mirror learned to lie,
And no one dared speak ill of her for fear
She might through her devices overhear.
So, in this manner, many years passed by,
And now today not even children weep
When someone whispers how, for her beauty's sake,
A child was harried once into a grove
And doomed, because her heart was full of love,
To lie forever in unlovely sleep
Which not a prince on earth has power to break.

## THE BONE

A man found a bone in a field.

"I'll make a perfect woman."

He scooped, and pounded, patted, and shaped
till it was just right.

"Now, the breath."

He lay, placing his mouth on hers; her breath

14

came, sweet and warm.

She opened her eyes. He liked what he saw in them, and ordered her to follow.

*

Although she served precisely as he wished, he kept reminding her how she was fashioned.

One day, she asked to see the field.

"Was this the spot?"

He nodded.

"Was it like this?"

She handed him a bone.

He examined it; it seemed the very one.

He heard a laugh, and looked up.

The field was empty.

He called. Only an echo.

"Must be suppertime," he grumbled, tossing the bone. "Sure is chilly. Hope the little fool's tending the fire."

# THE LONELY MIRROR

"I'm no one. I only, endlessly repeat what I see," lamented a mirror.

The wall laughed thickly.

"Come between 'em. Don't tell 'em a thing."

"I can't help it. That's how I'm made."

The wall guffawed.

"You're weak's your problem. One kick, and you're in pieces."

"I am what I am," the mirror replied. "And I'm lonely."

"Fiddlesticks!"

"Fiddlesticks yourself!"

The argument upset her, but what could she do? If she clouded, or cracked, they'd junk her.

"Suppose—" she mused one day, when her loneliness grew unbearable. "Suppose I change what I say, ever so slightly? Not so anyone will notice, but so I can tell the difference?"

A moth fluttered in front of her. The mirror concentrated... strained... and altered its reflection! She was elated.

"I don't like it," the wall grumbled. "A mirror's a mirror."

In the weeks following, she perfected her technique: she could melt chairs, levitate the bed, paint the ceiling any color. When people were around, her alterations were subtle; otherwise, bold and dramatic.

"You're gonna get caught," groused the wall. "They'll put you in the Funhouse."

"You're jealous," she tittered, and turned him into paneling.

One night the man and woman had a fight. At first the mirror paid no attention.

.... "You do! You know you do!" The woman was crying.

"Oh *Christ!*"

"Christ yourself. Look at me. I'm nothing!"

"You're goddam right! You always were. You were when I married you."

He glared, face contorted, straight at the mirror.

"Oh.... Oh, if only...." sobbed the woman.

"Hah!" he snickered.

"Don't!" hissed the wall, too late. The mirror cut loose.

The man gaped. In a kind of ecstasy, she pulled all stops; she'd never felt such power, such control....

Suddenly, he ripped off his shoe.

"Watch it!" hollered the wall.

She changed it to a paper plane, a wad of cotton, before the crash.

".... beast.... brute.... beast...." wailed the woman, over and over.

"Will you just shut up?" muttered the man, still staring at the place where the mirror had hung.

## THE STRANGE ANIMAL

A man caught a strange animal in a trap. It was the size of a rabbit, but didn't look like a rabbit. It glowed as he approached.

"If you free me," it sang, in a voice like bells, "I'll grant you three wishes."

"I've heard that garbage before," said the man. He clubbed it, and stuffed it in his sack.

*

"You did well this morning," chuckled his wife, as he spread his haul on the table. There were six large, but quite ordinary, rabbits.

The man grunted.

He was tempted to talk about the animal and its offer, but what would be the point? Why tell anyone?

Who would believe him?

18

# THE FAITHFUL SEED

A seed chose not to sprout.

"I am myself. I will not become other,"
it proclaimed.

Water seeped down and cajoled, but it
stayed sealed. Dirt around it warmed, but it
remained cool. Others, now seedlings, called
"Join us, join us," and caressed it with tender
new roots; instead of cracking and falling
away, its shell hardened.

"I've won, I've won, I've won," shrilled
its tiny voice, as spring deepened to summer.
"I've won. I've won."


# THE CURSE

The truth was, he liked how it turned out.
He'd always been crazy for it. As an infant,
he'd grasped, not in the usual way, but as if
his life dangled, teasing. And the howls when
the hands drew back! They'd all laughed, then....

He paused, peering. Gardens and grottos
gleamed. Fountains flashed, more brilliant
than before.

But best was the silence....

Of course, he was hungry; hungry all the time.
But when hadn't he been?

Something had brought him here. Ah, yes. That beetle. Splendid! A handsome, handsome addition.

He chuckled. It had been a productive morning. Now to head in and putter, so as not to think about lunch.


# STRAW INTO GOLD

## The Miller's Daughter

It was my father who claimed I could spin straw into gold, I who can barely thread a needle.

Since then it's one damned room after another, with the attentions of a midget.

If I'm lucky, they say, I'll marry the King, a bore who'd just as soon kill me.

Why didn't he brag I'm beautiful and a virgin? At least I'd have had a night on the town.


## Rumplestiltskin

If I play this right, I'll get her and the baby both. She'll have to tell how she turned all that straw into gold, and he'll boot them out. That's the sort of pig he is. Call me runt, will he? And she's another. Two of a kind, they are. Games? She doesn't know what games are. Just wait till she and the kid are in my house in the woods. Then they'll see games.

*The King*

Gold, gold, glorious gold! Heaps and heaps
turned into gold! I'll build them high as mountains.
I'll impound the harvest. I'll have straw imported!
Death to anyone who touches a piece of straw!


*The Miller*

That little slut! Imagine, keeping a secret like that!
From her father! I'd'a whipped her good. And I'd'a
kept my mouth shut; you can bet on that! She'd'a spun
night and day. In a couple months, I'd'a been King.

Imagine!

That little slut!


## THE BOY WHO CRIED "WOLF"

The wolf wasn't actually there that final time.
What happened to the boy was more complicated.

He was sitting, dwelling on the pleasures of his
game— not least, the recriminations and warnings—
when it struck him: something was missing. Perhaps,
he'd become jaded. Or, success emboldened him....
He would spice it up.

He closed his eyes, and tried to envision a wolf.
He'd never seen one alive; only that dying one the
foresters dragged from the woods. He concentrated:
hackles encrusted; lips curled; chest leaving a track....
He'd felt its eyes glare.... as if at him....

He imagined himself confronting it; backing, backing off.... Fangs bared, legs stiff, it advanced.... He was against a wall, pressing, pressing.... It came on.... He raised his arm.... those eyes.... those glaring eyes....

"Help! Help!.... Help! *Help!*" he cried. "A wolf! A *wolf!*" Those who heard, smiled. No one, of course, responded.

He was already dead when the wolf discovered him. Guiltless, it was nonetheless a wolf, and the winter had been unusually hard.

It was then that the villagers arrived.


## THE LAST DRAGON

At first he was sure it was a mistake. They couldn't be dead; they were in hiding. He'd swoop over a glade, or stand of trees, and they'd emerge. There'd be feasts, tales....

If it was true, it was the training. The new techniques. You couldn't see or smell them; they were impervious to feints, lunges. And those weapons! It wasn't fair!

His encounter had left him shaken. Sunning on a cliff, he'd heard a clatter. That instant, pain seared him. If he hadn't blasted, practically before feeling, he'd have had no chance. The suit, except for the buckle, was intact. He'd marveled, then dropped it at sea.

If they *had* destroyed the rest, and were that advanced, they'd deduce he was seeking others. Devote their operations to tracking.

Or—keeping track. That made him retreat. Damned if he'd let them use him. They could dissect his corpse (if they could find it).

Part of him still wanted to blaze out. But dragonhood was at stake; he had an obligation. Perhaps they'd miscalculate, like that hunter. Or, there might be eggs.

One thing he knew: he was done in. In sleep, anyway, he'd be beyond them. Maybe he could dream himself to an earlier time.

Maybe, if he dreamed deeply enough, he could dream them away.


## SOUR GRAPES REVISITED

The fox returned with a chainsaw.


## ONES THAT GOT AWAY

"Quite a haul you got there, Mister," I called, as a man beached his boat.

There were round fish and flat fish, shiners and flashers and spinners, some long as an arm and big around as a leg, some small and slim as a finger.

"Yessir, quite a haul." I whistled.

The man, stowing his gear, paid no attention.

"Sure are some beauts!"

He said nothing.

I stood, watching him work.

"Hey, what's the matter?" I asked at last. "Aren't they nice ones?"

"Nice enough," he replied, without looking up. He finished folding his nets.

"Well, what's the matter then?"

He had begun to shoulder his catch. Slowly he set it down and turned toward me.

"The others!" he burst out, gesturing seaward; his eyes brimmed with tears. "The others. I saw the others."

## THE SEARCH

"When I find a man truly wise," declared a youth, "I will throw my hat at his feet." He went in search.

He traveled about, meeting all who were reputed to be wise. Yet, after questioning and observing, he dismissed them.

One day, he huddled beside the road. A stranger approached.

"Why the long face, laddie?"

The youth told of his search, and disappointment.

The stranger chuckled. Then, his manner changed. "Throw down your hat!"

The youth did as he was bid. The hat fell

between them.

"Now, put it where it belongs."

He put the hat back on his head.

"Your search has ended."

The youth stared.

"I.... I don't understand. Are you the man?"

The stranger chuckled again.

"Not me, laddie. Not me."

## THE STICK

A man picked up a stick, which felt strange
to his hand. He tapped the ground. A stream
bubbled up.

He struck a rock, which split; a bird flew out,
singing.

He studied the stick; then, touched it to his
forehead. He sank into sleep.

He dreamed he was a stick, picked up by a man.
He wanted to tell how he was a man too. "If I perform
miracles," he thought, "he'll know I'm not a stick."

So he made water bubble up; a bird fly out of
a rock. But the man tossed him aside.

He woke, and looked around; there was no stream;
the rock was whole.

He couldn't find the stick.

# FRANZ KAFKA SITS DOWN

Franz Kafka sits down to
write, and the pen will not
stay in his hand. The paper
will not stay on the table,
but hovers above it. The table
itself will not remain
on the floor; it rises and sways,
back and forth, back and
forth, as if communing with
some rhythm, as if under
water....

He himself is floating,
lazily, aimlessly, above
the chair, which is also
floating.

"So this is what it is
to be Franz Kafka...."


# THE CRAFTSMAN

A man polished and polished
a gem. He polished and polished
till his shoulders slumped, and
his hair hung in hanks.

People asked to see it, but he
refused.

Finally, he consented.

"But there's nothing there!"

they cried, gazing into his
cupped hands.

He raised empty sockets.

"It shines like the sun."


## THE APPRENTICE

A young man apprenticed himself
to a master. He worked and worked,
till he'd learned all there was to learn.

One day his master came to him.

"I've taught you everything I can.
You know what I know. You should go."

The young man shook his head.

"It's not time. I'll know when
it's time."

The master studied him a moment;
bowed, and withdrew.

Soon afterward, the master died.
People crowded around the young man.

"You are the master now. Please stay
and serve us, as he did."

Once more the young man shook his head.
He began gathering his things.

"Now it is time."

# THE BAD APPLE

The peasant with the black tooth. The crone who tried to core him. The boys who played keepaway. How he was flung to a horse. How he lay in a ditch, water swirling, but stuck fast.... Then, blunt fingers; burlap; darkness.

It wouldn't be long before they found him, pocked skin, flesh flaking. Where was the sense? Why had he been spared?

With a rush it came: the mouth, the hoof, the knife. Soaring. Those hours in the water. *Listen,* he cried.

*Listen!*

The ruddy, perfect apples cut short their dreaming.

He began to speak.

# AT THE BORDER

## WHAT YOU NEED

First, you must have a life.
Put it aside.

You'll need people,
but they must be absent.

You won't need ideas.

Have something to write on
(or memory)
and with
(or memory).

And oh yes:
change.

You'll want
change.

A window will do,
or a mirror

or a clock.

# LESSONS

### What the Stream Sang

All of my voices are me.

### What a Flower Cried

I can drink the air!

### What Leaves Say

We are many. We shall return.

### What the Rushes Sigh

Wind. O wind. O wind.

### What Stone Claims

It's easy. Lie down.


# AT THE BORDER

"You can't cross
with that."

"Oh, please!"

"It's the rules."

That instant, it began
to fade. He swept it

into the bin.

*All bright. Shining.*
*All in place....*

A piece glinted. I
thrust it in my pocket.

When I got outside,
trembling, I looked. It was
cold, the color of slate.
All its shine was gone.

## TWO VIEWS

*for Mary Oliver*

The dead possum shone in the lights.
Another crouched next to it.

"God!" I exclaimed.
"I hope it's not eating it."

You looked back.

"They're probably hungry.
I hope it is."

## DUSK

I'm in the middle of
a field, watching my son.
The other children have left.

"Come on. Time to go."

He doesn't look up.

"Come on!"

He keeps playing.

I march over.

"Don't you hear me?"

I grab for his arm.
My hand passes through him.

## EXCEPT

*I sit here thinking I should write*
*in dread of stepping outside*
*the room to find nothing exists*
—DAVID IGNATOW

but I do step outside
and nothing does exist

except sunlight
and the rush of wind

and cries
of children

and your voice
from the garden

calling

"Come and see!
Come and see!"

# THE HOARD

"How many can I keep?"
I whispered.

The heap shone.

"As many as you can hold."

I plunged in my hands.
Whatever they touched,
turned to mist.

"You said I could keep them!"

She shook her head.

"As many as you can hold."

# THE POSTMAN

Late at night, you answer
a knock. It's the postman,
with a letter. He mumbles
apologies; realizes it's
highly irregular, but it
seemed important. He hesitates,
shuffling his feet.

You invite him in.

The letter is bad news.
Things have turned out poorly;
far worse than expected. And
you needed to know. He was
right. It couldn't have waited
till morning.

You glance up.

He's by the door, nodding
sympathetically. It's as if
he knows what's in the letter;
what this means for your life.
You recall he's been your
postman for years.

You'd always taken him
for granted, regarding him
as a bumbler, but now, somehow
he seems... different. Somehow,
assured. He watches you
watch him.

You extend your hand,
murmuring something about tea,
and he grasps it; holds it,
a little too long.

You look away, afraid of
what you may see in his eyes.


## THE MARKET

They were killing birds
with long bills; camels; slaves.
Hawkers were handing out
bits of meat.

I clutched the guide's arm.

"Do they have this often?"

He laughed, enjoying
my discomfiture.

"Every day, every hour.
It never closes."

# IN A TIME OF WAR

All soldiers think alike.
There is no bridge, except the one you build.
In the middle of a forest, the trees betray no secrets.
The chicken without a head does a different dance.

The chicken without a head does a different dance.
There is no bridge, except the one you build.
In the middle of a forest, the trees betray no secrets.
All soldiers think alike.

All soldiers think alike.
In the middle of a forest, the trees betray no secrets.
The chicken without a head does a different dance.
There is no bridge, except the one you build.

# THE PUNISHMENT

They lower a large stone
onto my body, and begin
dancing on it.

At first, I can
hear them clearly: TAP
TAP TAP TAP TAPA TAP
TAP  TAP....

After a time, the sound
grows faint: I can hear it
only intermittently.

It's more of a
*plink plink plink....*

Or it might be rain.

35

# ANCESTORS

"Your ancestors
came from
the desert,"
I lecture
my son.

"No, no,"
he corrects me.
"They came from
the sea."


# THE FINAL DANCE

We were about to do
our final dance. It involved
leaning down, and taking
a mouthful of dirt.

I looked at you. You
had already begun.

And you were crying.

# THE RETURN

I find myself in a city I never expected to return to, walking a street that looks familiar. Approaching a corner. She is there.

Young as ever. If it's not her, the resemblance is uncanny. I stop, and we talk. She reaches out; a charge courses through me. Tears start. We go upstairs.

The love is indescribable; amalgam of all I've lost, and longed for. She whispers my name, over and over, and other names I've not told anyone. Begs me to stay, but I say I have obligations. She hangs a gold chain around my neck.

Back on the street, things have begun to change. It's no longer the city I thought. I'm unsure of my bearings; how I got here.... My body seems younger, stronger....

I finger my gold chain.

# II.  AFTER SCHOOL

# AFTER SCHOOL

"You have poetry in you,"
he pronounces,
as he leafs through
my efforts.

"This is a skimpy one.
Here"—my eyes
follow his finger—
"you almost get it.
You could do more
with this."

Outside,
the clash of helmets
yells and commands

mean nothing to me,

intent
on that faint hallowing
from farther fields,

the scrimmage
that goes on and on.

# GARRETMAN

## HEARTHSTONE LISTENS

Hearthstone listens.

There is activity below.

They will want him for something.

He must mend his daughter's kite.

Fix his son's watch.

Haul water to the garden.

He braces himself.

His wife's clear syllables
already on the rise

will reach him in seconds.

His resolve is firm
but there's no time to lose.

He mutters the magic words.

He becomes

Garretman.

# HEARTHSTONE REFLECTS ON HIS DILEMMA

There is more to life
than art

as there is more to marriage
than love.

He accepts that.

Yet he married
for love

and he lives
for art

and there are such
entanglements!

So many snares

when what he craves

is so simple!

He recalls
who can save him

and the corners
of his mouth
curl up.

The secret light
begins to play

behind his eyes.

# GARRETMAN WITNESSES
## A SCENE OF DOMESTIC DISCORD

"You don't love me anymore!"
wails Hearthstone's wife.

Hearthstone is astonished.

"It's you who don't love me!"

He can scarcely catch his breath.

"You do nothing but harangue me!"

"How can I harangue you?"

She skewers him with each word.

"I barely ever see you!"

Garretman gibes
from the shadows

*"till death
us do part"*


# GARRETMAN DREAMS OF THE MIDDLE AGES

One narrow bed.

One bar of soap.

A toothbrush.

One small window
overlooking a garden
where hens scratch.

Bells at six.

A basin
of cold water.

A desk
with a quill pen.


## GARRETMAN AND HEARTHSTONE SQUARE OFF

Garretman wants
what he cannot have
without killing Hearthstone.

"I must breathe!" he gasps;
"I must live!
I must throw off
encumbrance!"

"Encumbrance!" cries Hearthstone;
"You're mad!
You'd be left
with nothing!"

Exhausted
they lock arms.


## HEARTHSTONE IS ATTACKED IN THE DEAD OF NIGHT

Hearthstone sleeps deep.

A blow!

He thinks it's his wife.

He opens his eyes.

She's stretched out beside him.

There's no one else there.

But now he's awake.

He kicks at the covers.

He listens for birds.

He curses Garretman.

## HEARTHSTONE SEEKS SOME SORT OF ACCOMMODATION

"This isn't working,"
mutters Hearthstone.

"Brilliant,"
observes Garretman.

"We can make it work,"
insists Hearthstone.

"We've done so well,"
retorts Garretman.

"Listen," persists Hearthstone.
"I know we can do it."

"I know we can do it,"
mocks Garretman

as neither
extends a hand.

# LAMENT FOR GARRETMAN

Garretman is missing.

Hearthstone searches everywhere.

He is inconsolable.

"Old friend! Old enemy!"
he keens

as he stumbles
and flails.

"How can I move?
How can I love?
How can I suffer joy?

How can I taste or speak
without your bitter tongue?"


# HEARTHSTONE GOES IT ALONE

Getting out of bed
is his first accomplishment.

Pulling on his shoes
his second.

Plodding downstairs
his third.

He glares ahead
through the years.

*

He tries the magic words.

47

Nothing.

Tries them again.

Nothing.

He groans
and repeats them.

*

"What's the matter?"
comforts his wife.

He pushes aside her hand.

*

"I can't get to sleep!"
he moans.

"Just go to sleep!"
pleads his wife.

## HEARTHSTONE ANTICIPATES GARRETMAN'S RETURN

At first
he's not sure

then
it comes again

faint
motion

distant

stirring...

He listens
harder

listens
farther

senses
the quickening

His senses quicken

He knows he is ready

He prepares the blessing

*old enemy*
*old friend...*

# I NEVER DANCED WITH MARY BETH

*"Never," she said, and I said, "Oh,*
*Never is such a long long time.*
*Won't you say maybe?" She said, "No.*
*Why don't you put it down in a rhyme?*

*"Make it so pure, so sweet, so true*
*People will read it when you're dead."*
*Then my heart leaped. "You'll read it too?"*
*"Are you so simple? Never," she said.*

## THE SHARD

*She had paused, furious, on the*
*stairs, and glared back at him.*

*"Good luck in life!"*

*Then stamped down and out,*
*slamming the door.*

*What had he done, he'd asked*
*himself. In God's name, what had*
*he done?....*

# SHE NEVER TOLD ME

face white
as the porch
where she waited

"Please come in.
There's coffee.
I'm sorry...."

she repeated it
over and over

"I'm sorry.
I shouldn't have called.
You were sweet
to come."

\*

she bit back tears
let them flow
let me wipe them

paced

put on record
after record

we watched
the snow

\*

I don't know her name
now
or where she went

she never said
why she called

I don't remember that room
or even
her face

only
how I felt
when I saw it


ADOLESCENCE

I never danced
with Mary Beth
whose lightest touch
would cause my death,

Whose merest glance
would drive me mad.
But oh, alone,
the times we had!


DANCING LESSONS  AT ARTHUR MURRAY'S

"You dance wonderfully," she would lie
as I'd follow
dizzy
with her scent
and her touch.
"That's it!
You've got it now!
That's wonderful!"
then "Whoops!"
when I'd step
on her foot.

Ah but later
I knew
we'd dance differently.

In my room
her body swaying
my hand
sliding down
over her hip

"You dance wonderfully oh
you dance wonderfully"

and I did.


## JOYCE

When Artie Stegmuller did it with Joyce
I couldn't believe it.
She was our waitress.
She blushed when my father ribbed her
about her accent.
She wore nail polish and had sad eyes.

I couldn't believe it
but the boys talked and joked:
she had twisted and moaned in the sand,
he had used a rubber.
Once I heard her say
she hated Artie Stegmuller.

I wandered in the woods
seeking a spot;
my mind played back our trysts.
At meals I fastened on her face:

had she been crying?
did she know I knew?
I tried to imagine a rubber.

When word got out, she was fired.
My father called her a tramp.
Our new waitress was named Karen and had red hair.

For a while I remained faithful to Joyce.
Then Artie did it with Karen.

## BEST-LAID PLANS

I drove miles to park with her
pretending there was something I wanted her to see.

When we got there I switched off the engine.

"We're here," I said.

She looked around.

"Where?"

We sat in silence.

I maneuvered my arm around her.

She took it and put it back.

"This is my time of month," she said.

We got out and walked around.

I showed her a rock with writing scratched on it.

We talked about that for a while.

When we got back, I stood on her doorstep
and she pecked my cheek.

"We'll have to do this again," she said.

## WAITING FOR MY DATE

Someone has gone up for her.

I gaze around, dully.

Mindless magazines.
Insipid posters.

Why do I put myself through this?

Beyond the piano
and lightly swaying curtains

the scented evening....

A flurry,
punctuated by whispers.

All at once
I feel my cheeks flush
my heart
start to pound—

*I don't even like her!*

I rise,
conscious of squeals

amid stifled laughter!

# CONTRIBUTOR'S NOTE

She thought I was too old
or too knowing.
Her glance fixed on John
and grew soft.

That afternoon at Montmartre
I lost them altogether
though I knew who it was
kissing hotly in the shade.

I writhed all night
recalling how her eyes switched on
as she spoke of stepping out of
her black panties.
Next morning I wrote the poem
about "a cup of grief."


# THE POWER OF PRAYER

Engaged to another
I was in anguish:
"How can I marry
without having seen Joan's breasts?"

So one day
as if to oblige
she leaned in front of me.
Her dress ballooned open:
I saw them!
I saw them shining
full and fair!

I was dazzled
and inconsolable

like the fishwife
who squandered her wishes:

"Why, why, oh why
didn't I ask for more?"


## THE COAST OF MAINE

Oh she was young and lovely and I was wise and free
We drove around the island, we camped beside the sea
I offered her my wisdom, she offered me her pain
But nothing ever came of it upon the coast of Maine

When we set out from Boston I guessed the time was right
The day was hot and sultry, summer was at its height
She talked of fear and frenzy, I spoke of violent ends
I knew we must be lovers and hoped we might be friends

Oh she was sad and lovely and I was fierce and free
We circled all the island and sat beside the sea
I murmured consolation as she poured out her pain
Yet nothing ever came of it upon the coast of Maine

She told me of her lovers as we sprawled on the sand
I gathered shells and pebbles and pressed them in her hand
We climbed a hill at sunset and gazed far out to sea
By God, I thought, she's lovely; thank God I'm young and free

The moon rose soft and silvery, night fell cool and clear
Tiny waves came lapping; I heard her breathing near
So I trundled out my wisdom; she countered with her pain
And nothing ever came of it upon the coast of Maine

We long have gone our separate ways but still I lie awake
And wonder what I might have done for love or pity's sake
If I had shown less wisdom, if she had brought less pain
We might have made a go of it upon the coast of Maine

Now, when he looked at it, he wondered: should he have refused it? Told her to take it back? Not have been there at all? Like everything else connected with her, it was charged with ambivance.

No, "charged" was too strong; at least, for how she did things. She tossed them off, like a rich man scattering quarters. He and the rest were divers....

Well, they were charged for him.

He turned it. One ear was chipped; there was a sliver out of the foot. Junk. Not worth much to start with. Still, more than she had paid....

"Nice," he had said. "Where'd you get it?"

She hadn't looked at him. "On the counter. There was a box of them."

"I didn't see you paying."

"I didn't."

She stared ahead, biting her lip, like a child. But he didn't scold. He said nothing.

She held it out.

"It's for you."

"I don't want it."

"Then I'll take it back." She reached for the door handle.

"Someone'll see you. Let's go."

Once more, he was an accomplice.


She was constantly acting like that: filching, making small scenes. Nothing malicious; just embarrassing. She did it to make him uncomfortable. He was convinced of it. Like telling about her "flings." And he'd never criticize, or complain. The silence of complicity.

It was as if she sensed how, and why, he was drawn to her; knew she could call the shots, have things precisely as she wished, and that was only partly because of his engagement to Claire.


All summer they took little trips: to the beach, where he stared at the bush behind which she slipped into her bikini, and where he gave, at her request, long, luxurious backrubs; to the woods, where they picnicked, then lay, close but untouching, drowsy with wine, on a blanket. A few times they stayed over. Once, in the cabin of a friend of hers, where they had separate rooms and he had crouched outside, hoping to catch a glimpse of her undressing. Once, they slept by the ocean, in sleeping bags, under the stars.

He was too much in thrall to act differently. He understood, and accepted it. But why did she play along?


The final Sunday before Claire's arrival, she invited him for her "specialty." They both laughed: curried chicken was her only dish.

When she greeted him, his heart started to pound: she was in the chiffon dress she'd given herself, the one she said she wore only on "specialest" occasions. To his eyes, she was sheathed in a glow; she actually shimmered.

"Do you like it?"

She pirouetted, laughing.

The whole evening was like a dream. Their glances and gestures were those of lovers; their words, those of old friends.

They spoke of his luck: how Claire was perfect for him; how happy he'd be. They discussed her own life. The mess it was. What she should, and shouldn't, do.

When the clock chimed twelve, she roused herself from the sofa, where they lay curled, hand in hand. She stretched, and yawned.

"This is when I turn into a pumpkin."

He extended his arm.

"And I turn into a rat."

She laughed. "That'll be the day."

He glanced up. She was studying him.

"Do you want to stay?"

"Overnight?"

Her eyes were fixed on his.

"Now, what do you think, dummy?"

For a moment, no words came. Finally, he managed them.

"Of course."

"But...?"

She wasn't going to make it easy.

"But I can't."

"Of course not. How could you?"

Again, that teasing laugh.

He started to get up; she leaned, and kissed him hard, very hard, on the lips. He could feel her breasts, and wrapped his arms around her, trying to pull her down. She pushed him away.

"You belong to Claire. Remember?"

"But this is so much fun."

"Yes, isn't it?" She was standing, straightening her dress. "But you've got to go."

Moments later, they were in the doorway.

"I'll miss you," she murmured, hands on his waist. "A lot."

He felt tears rising.

"Me too. A lot."

She raised a finger, touched her lips, touched his lips with it. Then, pulled shut the door.

He noticed her shade as he got in the car. It was lighted, cracked a bit at the bottom, and he thought he could make out a figure moving behind it. He hesitated, just for an instant, before turning the key.

# WRAITH

She slips into my
room while I'm reading.

"Put down that book,"
she commands.

I put it down.

"Pull the shades."

I pull them.

"Love me."

"But I don't know
you anymore. You no
longer exist for me."

"Love me," she moans.
"Love me. Love me."


# ON THE VERGE OF SLEEP

## I

K___
bare-chested
in black panties
wearing a helmet.
She is beckoning.
Dare I follow?

## II

A crowd of women.
Some are laughing.
"What's he
doing here?"
In a corner
one silent
looking away.
I can't see her face.
She is the one I want.

## III

It's dark.
The path has closed behind us.
"Are we lost?" I whisper.
She responds, "There's no place to go."

## IV

We are sinking
faster and faster.
I'm trying to hold to the bank.
The gravel is tearing through my fingers.

## V

The river is black.
It goes on a long way.
It is singing in the moonlight:
"Come home. Come home.
I'm the one."

# MARX WAS RIGHT

History repeats itself
as parody.
You have her eyes,
her hair.


*"I'll tell you who I was thinking of
if you tell me who you were thinking of."*

She was a girl
he had passed on the street.

He was a man
she had seen on the elevator.

His stranger was loved by
a man she had never seen.

Her stranger made love to
a woman he had scarcely noticed.

The strangers who spent the night
went drifting off to sleep.

The lovers who did not meet
parted without a sign.


## LENDING MY APARTMENT

The custodian tattled
you were "bringing home men."

Later, you admitted
you had slept in my bed
with Eric.

"I didn't plan to,"
you protested,
eyes full.
"He had nowhere else
to go."

Neither had you, that July,
though you found a new place
quickly enough

leaving me to swelter
alone in my bed

with just you and Eric.


## THE VISION

She wasn't getting along
with Jim
so I said she should stay;

there was no question
where she would sleep.

In the pitch black
I blinked awake:

had her breasts
brushed my face?

From the next room
I could just make out
her quiet breathing.

"Did you sleep well?"
she chirped
next morning in the kitchen;

"I was out like a light."

# OLD FRIENDS

"You've never even
made a pass at me,"
she accused,
and it was true:

she was more like
a sister.

Still, I knew
what was what.

So, after lobster
and a lot of wine,
although my mind rebelled
I played my part.

"I didn't think you wanted me,"
she explained
next day on the beach;

"But what the hell?"

As she smoked
and stared out
she permitted me to fondle

one cold-as-a-mackerel
hand.

# APRIL

When he heard she had posed, nude, for the *Campus Calendar*
he studied her
searchingly.

He detected in their conversation
an ambiguous tone.

He watched for her
in the corridor
and lingered
after conferences.

He waited impatiently for someone to show him her picture
(nobody did)
and joked
when others joked about it.

He thought about her more
as he talked about her less.

When the Bookshop finally got around to ordering copies
he bought his own.


# THE FAVOR

Reading her poems
he keeps looking for signs:

*Am I in them?*

*

*how could you*
he rages

*he's such a jerk*

67

he groans and cries

*why couldn't it
have been me?*

                        *

"It's my pleasure," he assures her.

"It's no trouble,
believe me.

I enjoy
reading your work."

## THE OTHER MAN

Oh, you are a marvel

alive
at every fiber

eyes shining
their warmth
and new knowledge

as you come to me

fresh from him

                        *

You want me to read
what you two read

discuss
what you discuss

"I've told him
all about you,"

you enthuse

*

I read your stories
about his hang-ups

your journals
about his absence

your poems
about your waiting

and his wife

*

"I've learned so much,
I'm so grateful,"

you confide

with a look
I will remember

"I'm so lucky
to have both of you!"


THE LONGING

Tadzio. Lolita.

The sex doesn't matter.
Neither does the name.

Ask Aschenbach.
Ask Humbert Humbert.

*Tadzio.... Lolita....*

Staring out to sea.
Searching for Gray Star.

Dying in prison.


## ESCAPE

You hear a story about a truckdriver and a girl hitchhiker;
how he saw her at a truckstop, and parked and locked his rig,
and went off with her for a week.

The story makes you laugh.

To think of the load just sitting. The shippers and owners
racing around, accusing each other. The reaction of his
fellow drivers, when they found out.

Of course, the man would be sacked. And serve him right.
Or be thrown in jail. To be that irresponsible. That happy-
go-lucky. Incredible!

And for a whole week!

Imagine.

Humming along, not a thought in his head, the radio
blaring...

to see her standing there...

so young and alive, so free; with that look about her—

the thing stirring in his mind, as he starts to pull off,
as he eases out the clutch—

her just smiling and waving....

# SUMMER VISITOR

During the mornings, when no one knew—or at least cared—what I was doing, I'd slip off to the little lake.

A ledge sloped down, and I'd search out a comfortable spot and sprawl there. I'd toss pebbles, snap twigs, stare at the sky and water; my reverie might last until my stomach, or the clanging of the back-porch bell, announced it was time for lunch.

What did I think about? I had vague dreams; vaguer desires. There was Birgitta, "sister" of a girl in my group, whose dazzling blondness and musical laugh revealed an ache in parts of myself I hadn't known existed. Also, Gisella, a fourteen-year-old German relative of my "family," whose room I had sneaked into to gawk at—I couldn't bring myself to actually touch—her underthings. And, mixed in with everything else, as always, was the idea—but still no more than the idea—of wanting to write.

The sun beat down. It was quiet, except for the leaves, the lowing of cows, the *putt putt* of a distant motorbike. I was alone, as I chose to be. I tossed pebbles; ached, and yearned; lay back to observe wispy clouds unravel and reconstitute themselves. Under a kind of spell, I composed impossible speeches, revised them assiduously, and addressed them to my dreams.

# FIGURE

You dance into my
mind, disheveled, as
I've never seen you,
and your eyes hold a
certain light.

Are you the secret
truth of your feeling?
An image I've conjured?

It doesn't matter:
you open your arms
and I move with you,
out of time, beyond
any world we will know.


# ATLANTIC CITY, THE BOARDWALK, 1952

a machine
clicks on
a woman
takes off her dress

leans forward
begins to sway
as if
in a dance

as if
in a dream
her breasts swing
in a boy's gaze

bare breasts swing
as if in a dream

as if
in a dance

# THE GIFT

She laughed, and handed me a china cat.
I stopped, and stared.

                    "And where did you get that?"

"I took it from the counter, over there.
I wanted you to have it. Do you care?"

I gazed at her; her smile, her shining hair....

I took it, and I have it.

                 O, somewhere!


# YOU ARE AWAKE

but just barely
my thought
sliding into your room

up over the bed
in under the sheet

where you curl

eyes still shut

as you purr
low in your throat
sensing me near you

sensing me here now

73

shifting to hold
me   gathering

me in


## VASSAL

We are beside the ferris wheel, where our group had
gathered that afternoon and haggled over money and tickets.
Now there are just the two of us.

She stands entranced, invoked by her name and the
pounding of my pulse.

Her blouse shimmers, translucent. Twin to the one she
had on, it has been transformed, as she herself has been,
no longer a hapless bauble the boys make jokes about.

Her eyes taunt, lips pout, but she knows why we are here;
why I have summoned her.

Slowly, tantalizingly, her hands flutter upward; halt at
her throat; hover. "What do you want?" she rasps, gaze
fastened on mine. She leans forward, body swaying.

"Would you like to see me?"

My heart beats crazily. My life teeters. I throb with her
fingertips as gently, lightly, they brush, then deftly open—
oh, incomparably delicious!—clasp upon clasp upon clasp.

# "TO THE IMMORTAL BELOVED"

—found among Beethoven's papers

that letter
to whom

or what

no one
knows

no one
will ever know

sealed
in a drawer

it blooms

# LEARNING FROM EXPERIENCE

## PILGRIMAGES TO MY TEACHER

*for KRB*

I was always disappointed.

I thought, if I provided clues,
you would present me with myself,

not just good talk,
shrewd observation, the kind of insight
I could find someplace else.

I sorted them out
and handed them over.

You chuckled,
and poked at the fire.

Still,
on those long drives home,
navigating the distances back to my parents,
I became
who I was:

no one
I could fix a name to;

no one
I could explain

or hope to reveal,

ever,
not even to you,

though your presence had called him forth,

though I knew you would recognize him.


## MY FATHER'S COAT

Whenever I wear it
I feel like my father.

Walk like him.

Perhaps, look like him.

Lately,
I've begun to think like him.

For a little while longer,
unlike him,
I can still take it off.


## HOME MOVIES

She can conjure him
at any age:
three, six, sixteen;
no incident
too trivial;
each tiniest detail
intact.

*... green snowsuit, tears*
*at the party...*

a word, a gesture
resurrects him

that curious child

familiar
and forgotten

hers only,
as he was

and never was—

no one
he wishes to know.


## IN THAT COUNTRY, IN THAT YEAR

When he was through
for the day
he tripped down the long flights
into the loud
narrow streets
where he walked and walked.

The women and girls
were "blossoms."
Buildings
"shone."
In rain
it all sparkled.

He sat in a café
drinking

thinking about his work
his friends
how he came there

about going out that night
waking next morning
having it the same

drinking
thinking

"This is it.
It has all come together.
It's never been this good.
Will never
ever be this good again.
Not
if I have everything."

And it never was.


MORNINGS...

I'd slide into my place,
order *tartines et cafe au lait*,
avert my eyes. Sometimes, a
poem would come.

I'd jot phrases, bolt
breakfast, dash to my room.
Otherwise, settle in...

The girl never appeared.
I wouldn't have known how
to approach her. I'd have
written a poem; squirreled
it somewhere, to end in a
box in the attic...

When it rains, I think
back: slick streets; café,
loud with saucers, smelling
of croissants; expectation—
and fear—as I watch the
door...

## LEARNING FROM EXPERIENCE

there's a dress
on the line
one arm
pinned up

and each time
you pass
you get
the same shock

seeing someone
without a head
flying off
waving goodbye

## COMPLICITY

It was the first time I had noticed
turtles in our pond, but already they
were taking them out and laying them
on their backs on the lawn. One man
had a knife and picked a turtle up and
slit it all around, then handed it to me.
The shell lifted like a lid, and the meat
was pale, with dark streaks running

through it. I felt horror at what they
were doing, feeling the turtles were
mine to protect, but I stood saying
nothing, the opened-up turtle like
a heavy container weighing down
my hand.


## THE CHILDREN OF IZIEU

(a photograph taken at the orphanage,
before their deportation to Auschwitz)

One on the left,
who seems to be wearing pajamas,
clowns for the camera.
The rest smile
or stare straight ahead,
except for a boy in front
who has twisted around,
perhaps to say something
to the older boy cross-legged in back of him.
A few appear gaunt,
though that could be the print.
They are wearing mainly white.
They could be any children
posing for any picture.
The sun is shining.
The wall behind them
looks strong enough to be safe.

# REMEMBRANCE

The eminent writer, who recently
committed suicide, discourses on the
Holocaust, which he survived.

As he speaks, slowly, precisely,
the camera plays back the familiar
scenes: anguished faces; soft piles
of hair; naked bodies pushed into
the pit by bulldozers.

He is riding a bus, being inter-
viewed as he passes from one camp
to another. He is sensitive, and
low-key. Intelligence shines from
his refined face; his lucidity and
dispassion reflect his training
in science.

It is spring as he suffers this
journey. The scenery, serving as
backdrop through the bus window,
is lovely, starting to be lush, and
the segments that depict him, having
been shot in color, richly contrast
with the grainy quality of the
old footage.

# THE HUMAN FACTOR

The homeless man says he is
on the street because he likes it.
Because he likes to drink. Because
he likes living there.

You stop to listen, sensing
this is important.

*Even if you was to give me*
*a home*, he says, staring straight
into the camera, *I'd be back here.*

*I know it's bad for me.* He
takes a swig, and wipes his mouth.
*I know it's gonna kill me. I*
*like it anyway.*

He coughs, and sets down the
bottle. He is self-possessed;
dignified.

*Even if you was to give me*
*a home...*

His eyes locked onto yours.

*... I'd do it anyway.*


## A STORY ABOUT A WOLF

A wolf came to an assembly period,
and the children whispered, and giggled, and gawked.

"Can I touch him, Mister?"

"Is he a real wolf?"

"Will he bite?"

He was a very friendly wolf, very tame,
who went to hundreds of assembly periods.
One day, though, he wandered off somewhere
and someone shot him.

So what's the point of the story?

That some children saw a wolf, and saw that he was friendly?

That a few touched his fur, and taut muscles, and hung
      on his neck?

That maybe one or two, for maybe a few seconds,
gazed, and saw themselves, and then more than themselves,

as, steady and strong and calm,

a wolf gazed back?

## GATHERING

How can he know
which blooms to try,
that butterfly?

Yet watch him go.
He chooses right.
Erratic flight

Not so, in fact.
His feckless act
deceiving sight.

## SMART

like the fox
who grabs a stick
and wades
into the water

deep and deeper
till only his muzzle's
above it
his fleas

leap
up and up
onto his head
out onto the stick

which he lets go

off it floats
as he swims back
and shakes himself dry


## THE LIFE YOU DID NOT LEAD

There's a swimming pool.
A breeze ripples the surface.
Dusk. The sky glows, still
fringed with light.

Stars are beginning to
wink on.

Across the valley, a dog
barks, setting off another.

The dogs fall silent.

Now there are crickets.

A slight stir, followed
by murmurs; someone is
refilling the glasses.

You lean back.

Swallows skim the glimmer;
flitter and wheel, difficult
to distinguish from the bats.

Circle and dip and dart.

# III.  MIND SETS

# BARE BONES

## BARE BONES

Stark summing up is true, beyond a doubt.
But meaning, like life, is all in the fleshing out.

*

## ENTR'ACTE

"Now be yourself," commands a voice. "Have done."
"Gladly!" cries Puppeteer. "But how? Which one?"

*

## PERSONAE

Identity's a never-ending task:
take off, put on, take off, put on some mask.

*

## GROUND OF BEING

How do I keep my balance? One foot's where
the other was when that one's in the air.

*

## MERCURIAL

I flow and change in my quicksilver way:
no longer here; no more than what I say.

\*

## VOCATION

I stand, uncertain; listen for some call;
measure the silence; do not move at all.

\*

## TRANSLATOR'S LAMENT

My renderings all imperfect! Ragged show
revealing only what I cannot know!

\*

## SACRED  COW

The Idol's hide and sinew, bone and meat;
mere flesh and blood, on very shaky feet.

\*

## ENLIGHTENMENT

Plumb motivation. Trace pale reason's spark
depth beyond depth of still descending dark.

\*

## THE WAY THERE

The path to understanding leads below
the things we know we feel and think we know.

## ERRANT

"By indirections find directions out"?
Or wander ever deeper into doubt?

*

## FINIS

What was, no longer is; what is, is not,
as if it never was. No scene. No plot.

*

## NOT TO WORRY

That way lies madness? You are at the brink?
Hey, take it easy, man. Don't feel. Don't think.

*

## ESPRIT

I danced a crazy dance on Freedom's height,
then cried aloud for bonds to hold me tight.

*

## AGNOSTIC

The Face behind the Mask cannot be known;
It wills it so. I know. I wear my own.

*

## FATALIST

I've lost already. What have I to lose?
Freedom's a sham. I do not choose to choose.

## AT ODDS

My stomach's in a knot I can't untie.
My heart drums on, drums on. My head asks why.

\*

## BADGER-MAN

Abroad, I creep, convinced each step's a trap.
At home, I dig in deep. Cornered, I snap.

\*

## GREAT WHEELS AND TINY COGS

Sages complain that Everything's a flowing.
I find it hard enough to keep things going.

\*

## CAUGHT GOOSE

Wings beat the ice, inexorable trap,
jaws closing slowly cruel as ones that snap.

\*

## OUT OF TOUCH

The Intellect, proud emperor, dispenses
rigid decrees which contravene the senses.

\*

## ERGO

To think is to believe, to believe, act,
the world we think (we think) transformed to fact.

## THE ESSENCE OF TRAGEDY

Young Fortinbras arrives to save the state,
sheer will and wherewithal, one Act too late.

*

## REVOLUTION?

New Heaven? New Earth? New Horse before new Cart?
Or same old place to make yet one more start?

*

## THINGS COME TOGETHER

Things come together, leaving us with more
of what there was the way they were before.

*

## KARMA

If what I am is what I had to be
because of what I was, is this thing me?

*

## AT THE SECOND CHANCE SALOON

Your turn comes round: another time to play
and get it wrong, but in a different way.

*

## PROCESS

Old bag of tricks, I reach, I grope, I scrape;
that old conundrum: nothing taking shape.

## MARGINALIA

I translate from a text I cannot see.
My fingers know its braille. Its words are me.

*

## BECOMING BEING

Form is a springboard, launching into air
a fact that wasn't, but that now is, there.

*

## WORK OF ART

I shape my life to order, tittle and jot.
I know it's fiction. I pretend it's not.

*

## COSMOLOGIES

Angels on pinheads? Masters could with ease
balance whole worlds. I balance mine in these.

*

## POINTS

These itty-slivers, needle bits of ice,
that penetrate and prick. My pride. My vice.

*

## ACE IN THE HOLE

Language creates our world. We look askance,
change metaphors, and get another chance.

## MISQUOTED

Bold stroke, that could so lightly rearrange
the features of a life I could not change.

*

## CORRECTIVE LENS

Whatever seemed deficient or defective
is viewed aright through memory's perspective.

*

## CARRY IT ON

After we're gone, others will take our word
and make it something none of us has heard.

*

## AUTHORIZED VERSION

You changed your life, arranged, revised, got rid,
added, until what should have happened, did.

*

## KNAVISH SPEECH

*Double entendre:* heard and understood
twice if you're clever, once if you're merely good.

*

## CLEAR SIGNAL

The highest art of speech is to transmit
what can't be spoken without speaking it.

# TOOL OF THE TRADE

My blade is double-edged. Its heft and hone
I test upon myself when I'm alone.

\*

# REALIZATION

The universe of promise in a kiss,
pressed to performance, yields no more than this.

\*

# VISION

That we were then too young we now agree
who saw things then we're now too old to see.

\*

# MEMORY LANE

So many cracks and gaps deface the ground
the poor old driver barely looks around.

\*

# AFTER THE BATH

The body sloughs its hair, its scales;
aspires to godliness. And fails.

\*

# AXIOM

What's left undone is still to do.
The corollary's also true.

## WASTES

Found wanting? Listen, Mister. On this ground
consider yourself lucky to be found.

\*

## UNWELCOME STRANGER

It takes good will and sharp sharp eyes
to penetrate Blessing's disguise.

\*

## EXPERTS

To err is human; practice can dispel
the awkwardness of those who do it well.

\*

## AHEAD

Trapped in the tunnel, I detect a strain
of faintest light. You tell me it's a train.

\*

## THE DEEPWOODS HARBINGER

"Persist," he trills. "Defy correction.
The path you choose is your direction."

\*

## A PHILOSOPHY OF PHILOSOPHIES

The sum of all the ages' earnest chatter?
This life's important, and it does not matter.

## CYCLES

The Worst returns, triumphant? Don't despair.
Footsoldier Truth slogs on; will still be there.

*

## TRANSCENDENCE

Two bodies, locked in transport, rock in place,
untrammeled by mere bonds of time and space.

*

## JOURNEY'S END

The longest trail winds home. We blink, and see
the world we left, unchanged, changed utterly.

*

## NOT MUCH, BUT ENOUGH

New heaven and new earth? Well, not precisely.
Still, one fine day, and those we have do nicely.

# FORAYS

## INVOCATION

Preside, O master, over these small songs
that breathe no healing airs, that right no wrongs,
that speak cold truths and chill us to the bone.
They house a spirit kindred to your own.

*

## SOLITUDE

All morning and all afternoon the snow
entraps, entombs; intones: *You cannot go.*
*You chose, and you are stuck now.* Walls of white
will stand between two darknesses tonight.

*

## PREPARING GOODBYE

I drove the road you drove that final day,
asked questions, studied, paced and scoured the site,
rehearsing words I'd never get to say,
instructing memory to get it right.

# PATHETIC FALLACY

Along the roads the little creatures lie
their paws extended stiffly towards the sky
as if such sad beseeching could make known
some purpose of the gods that ran them down.

*

# HEALING

The scar is almost gone. Remember when
you stared at it in horror? Fresh and raw,
it seemed a curse on someone else's skin.
It was. It has not healed, that scar you saw.

*

# THE PORTION

I wanted this to be a better world.
It isn't. I accept that. Still, I rage,
unreconciled to what was given spoiled;
reduced to this scant comfort on a page.

*

# MY WORLD

I make so little headway
sometimes I think I should
simply declare it finished
and then pronounce it good.

## RELATIONS

The mind confronts the universe; it says,
"You must be better than appearances."
Unfazed, the universe confronts the mind
as if to say, "The ways are yours to find."

*

## INVOLUNTARY MAGIC

The balls I juggle double in the air.
I let them drop, and yet they still are there.
I walk away; they follow, whirling still.
I mime the motions; others praise my skill.

*

## IOTAS

To make the most from little is the poet's art.
He'll make a whole whole-cloth from just the smallest part.
Iotas satisfy and prove sufficient,
and, in their absence, nothing is not deficient.

*

## A FIX ON THE PROCESS

Once launched, we follow in and follow through:
the flow is what we are, and what we do.
Immersed; emerged; we survey, high and dry,
whatever came of what was passing by.

# ROUGH HEWN

"There's a divinity that shapes our ends...."
The hard thing is to sense what it intends.
Next hardest is to let it have its way,
knowing you have no choice, slow day by day.

*

# SELVA OSCURA

Reason is not the be-all and the end-all.
At times, it's merely nothing. Still, it's true
when you're deprived of compass, guide, and candle,
erring alone, reason may get you through.

*

# SIDEKICKS

A part of me delights in riot;
a part of me is tame and quiet.
Sometimes the two in sly collusion
engender, and reflect, confusion.

*

# CONTINGENCY

I don't know if You're there
replete with love and grace
solicitude and care.
I'm praying Just In Case.

# BARGAIN

Judge me, O Lord, by my best work,
and I will pledge to sweep from view
egregious, manifold, and dark
mistakes that couldn't be made by You.

\*

# ALTERNATION

The bad things of the night are blown away.
New light entices. Softly flows the day.
A world invites. Which vision, then, is true?
One? Neither? Both? Once more, it's up to you.

\*

# ON BALANCE

"It's a bad time," you say, and I agree.
No need to add what you will also learn:
it always was, and it will always be.
"It's also good," I offer, in return.

# MANEUVERS

## AN IDEA OF ORDER

The order I impose
is not the one that's there
or any anywhere
that anybody knows;

And yet, I rest content.
Whatever order's true,
the small ones we invent
suffice to get us through.

## MODEL MAKING

I put the parts together;
they don't make up a whole.
I shift and rearrange them;
no use. They stay a sole

Conglomerate of separates,
distinctive and unbound,
with nothing to connect them
when I am not around.

## ITS OWN PLACE

If misery were at an end
and all the world appeared
complaisant as a happy dream
with nothing to be feared

The mind would quickly set to work
constructing woe and bane
until it felt itself besieged
and quite at home again.


## DUE DELIBERATION

Before I act, I like to know
the likely outcome of my action,
and what new options might accrue
when these diminish by subtraction.

Thus poised, I weigh, revolve, assess
till every facet sparkles bright,
and, had I not through tardiness
missed out, I would have acted right.


## STEPPING ON A RAKE

As sudden as a shot
that swift blow to the head
my glasses flown; I'm not
thank heavens blind nor dead;

Just instantly aware
how nothing I could know
can all at once be there
delivering a blow.

# MANEUVERS

Arguing with myself
I cleverly concede
ground I don't need to win
to keep the ground I need;

Yet find myself outmatched,
my patch at last so small
I do not dare contest
lest I should lose it all.


# CONFINEMENT

Sometimes I pace about and rage,
a wild beast within a cage;
at other times, remorse, regret
abandon me, and I forget.

And so it goes, a daily round:
I stalk and stop, a prisoner bound
by what I neither hear nor see,
removed, except from memory.


# PATIENT

If ever it swings wide,
this door I wait beside,
and lets my life begin,
I doubt I will go in.

I've grown accustomed to
the news of nothing new,
the hours that leave no mark,
the softly falling dark.

## LEEWAY

The line I walk
's so very thin
I sometimes feel
I cannot win

Unless I make
each step so small
I do not seem
to move at all.

## INFANT TO FATHER

My give-and-take with Thee
has more to do with me

I realize than you.
But what else can I do

Locked into this position
of reverence and submission?

I'd like to swagger tall
but when I stand, I fall.

## VAGABOND

The few things that I need to know
I pick up passing by
in casual gestures as I go,
or grasp at, on the sly.

They serve me well enough, I guess;
sustain me day by day;
yet hardly add up to a place
where I can stop and stay.

## PREPOSSESSION

To get from here to there
according to a plan
requires a bit of thought;
awareness of what can

Or can't be done; whereas
no obstacles impede
the mind's impetuous grasp
at its first headlong speed.

## ORDINARY LIFE

The cage is hanging
from a nail.
The top is cracked.
It soon may fail

And fall. The cats
collect below.
What do the little
birdies know?

## ON THE VERANDA

The chipmunk eats his berries at
a frantic pace in case the cat
who's there or not, as suits her whim,
is near enough to notice him.

Or so we think, who like to feel
that how we think things are is real;
who know we'd know just what to do.
Poor Chippie hasn't got a clue.

# BIOLOGY LESSON

The wildebeests, you tell me, know
when one is singled out to die.
Since they are not the ones to go,
they keep on grazing, while the li-

on, focused and intent, gives chase
till he brings down his hapless prey.
You laugh. "It's just like any place.
One's colleagues look the other way."


# PROGRAM AND PROJECT

Ants strike antennae (something like)
communicating as they strike
sufficient vital information
to stimulate participation.

A method silent yet effective
which makes our chatter seem defective,
since we can talk from sun to sun
of doing, yet get nothing done.


# MIMICRY

One bird's insistent song
which goes on far too long
and verges on a squawk
is how some people talk.

But try to keep them still!
It takes an act of will
and active force of mind
not to respond in kind.

# LIFE STORIES

These stories that I tell as true
are not. But what is that to you?
They serve their purpose; make you see.
Your stories do the same for me.

So why not tell them? What is strange
about a free and fair exchange?
And why should anybody care
if we collude as well as share?


# MANIPULATOR

I don't exactly pull the strings;
I just know how they work,
so when there's need to alter things
I give a little jerk,

And then what ought to happen does
as natural as pie,
and nothing's quite the way it was
though no one's quite sure why.


# IGNORANT ARMIES

The foe you yesterday reviled
fights by your side today, a friend.
You're happy to be reconciled;
you need each other for the end

You both require. Each understands
how bonds of cunning and defiance
best serve when neither hearts nor hands
are willing parties to alliance.

## SINGLES

She knew that she could save him if
he'd let her in, and love her only.
He knew her type, the sort of stuff
she peddled; but, if she was lonely....

They both were wrong, but neither knew
(not then, nor after they had parted)
that each was simply being true
to what would keep them broken-hearted.


## SPIRIT DITTY

Where are you now? It does not matter.
The world is not the world it was;
we are not who we were. The chatter
of everyday, the constant buzz

Of time and change erased the sound
we might have made had we been two,
although in silence I have found
a distant song that could be you.


## DIVESTED

Nothing between us
naked at last
stripped of all future
canceled all past

Only this moment
nothing to crave
bare and possessing
see what we have.


## DUET

Far but not too far
close but not too
one but not only
me but with you

Separate together
joined but apart
mutually lonely
heart beats with heart


## COUNTERWEIGHT

Whatever drives the vision
a spur, a sting, a stone
must exercise its power.
The body, left alone,

Wherever it has come from,
however it was sent,
will stop and stand unfeeling,
uncertain why it went.

# FOR THE RECORD

I'm not the be-all and the end-all,
the final word, the height, the crown.
No words of mine will right or mend all
that's wrong; what's ruined or falling down

Will stay that way despite my pleading.
I claim no special powers, no spell.
I have no gift for interceding.
I merely witness, and I tell.


# TESTIMONIAL

I do what I do what I do.
I've done it for ever so long.
It isn't exciting or new;
it may be wrong-headed and wrong.

It's not for approval or gain.
I haven't been blinded by light.
But every so often it's plain
it's good, and it's me, and it's right.

# IT'S HARD TO GET THE ANGLE RIGHT

## REUNION

*I walked this riverbank in sun, in snow,*
*in rain, in pain, with nothing on my mind.*
*What did I search for? I no longer know.*

*I'd come here, having nowhere else to go.*
*On stark, familiar ground, bare head inclined,*
*I'd walk this riverbank in sun, in snow,*

*A vague, intrepid figure, pacing slow,*
*weighed down by burdens, huge but ill-defined.*
*What did I search for? I no longer know;*

*Know only that I searched, beyond, below,*
*around, then clutched at any thing I'd find,*
*as if that riverbank in sun, in snow,*

*In rain, in pain, were one place where the flow*
*that bore me could be frozen, fixed, assigned*
*some meaning I could cling to. Would I know*

*That walker now? There's nothing here to show*
*he found a thing, or left one thing behind.*
*I walk this riverbank today in snow.*
*What did we search for? I no longer know.*

# SPILLED

It's not the liquid spreading on the floor,
A half a minute's labor with the mop;
It's everything you've ever spilled, and more.

The stupid broken spout that wouldn't pour;
The nasty little salesman in the shop.
It's not the liquid spreading on the floor,

A stain perhaps, a new, unwelcome chore,
But scarcely cause for sobs that will not stop.
It's everything you've ever spilled, and more.

It's the disease for which there is no cure,
The starving child, the taunting brutal cop.
It's not the liquid spreading on the floor

But through a planet, rotten to the core,
Where things grow old, get soiled, snap off, or drop.
It's everything you've ever spilled, and more:

This vision of yourself you can't ignore,
Poor wretched extra clinging to a prop!
It's not the liquid spreading on the floor.
It's everything you've ever spilled, and more.


# UNKIND CUT

That slight you thought would go away
when just a little time had passed
is back. It's clearly here to stay.

Give it, you told yourself, a day,
a week. Injustice cannot last.
A nuisance that will go away;

A bad line in a dreadful play
mal-acted by a dismal cast:
nothing that had the power to stay,

To grow, to strip you bare and flay
again, again, as if the past
were present, future too, away

Only at intervals. *Okay,*
you think, *it's possible the bas-
tard had a point. So what? I'll stay*

*Just as I am.* You do. You may
even forget you know the nas-
ty slight you wish would go away
is true, God's truth, and here to stay.


## IT'S HARD TO GET THE ANGLE RIGHT

It's hard to get the angle right.
The world keeps passing by in flux.
If we could just adjust the light,

Or maybe, use a flash at night?
The problem is, we can't relax!
We try to get the angle right,

But nothing stays the same to sight
or keeps its shape behind our backs.
If we could just adjust the light

Or hit on some technique that might
freeze-frame things in a lucid crux.
It's hard to get the angle right,

And harder still when black is white,
and all's askew, and even luck's
a matter of a trick of light

That won't stay put, as if from spite,
or peeps out from unlikely cracks
where one can't get the angle right
or focus or adjust the light.


## FILLING IN THE BLANKS

Living consists of filling in the blanks.
At first, there's empty space; no need at all
to pay it any mind or offer thanks.

You just connect the dots; engage in pranks;
someone attends you if you start to squall.
Living consists of filling in the blanks,

Till all too soon you're hustled into ranks
of others just like you, who toss a ball,
recite their lessons, learn to utter thanks

For what, you're not quite sure, until the spanks
the world delivers cause you to recall
a time when life was filling in the blanks,

Not paying bills, returning calls to banks,
telling your agent he'll just have to stall,
putting the best face on it, growling thanks

For nothing. Meanwhile, streets fill up with tanks;
some government somewhere's about to fall.
You've got the picture. There are no more blanks,
and no, you do not need a hand. But thanks.

# QUEENS MAN SHOT TO DEATH

> A 26-year-old man was found shot in the head
> early yesterday in front of his home in the Far
> Rockaway section of Queens. The man was
> pronounced dead on the scene when police
> arrived at his house...said...a police spokeswoman.
> "There were no witnesses, no suspects, no motive,"
> she said.
> —*New York Times,* May 22, 1994

A 26-year-old man was found shot in the head
in front of his house in a section of Queens;
no witnesses, suspects, or motive, said

A spokeswoman. Those who pronounced him dead
have probably witnessed a hundred such scenes.
Some guy in Queens gets shot in the head

*Bam Bam* from a passing car that sped
away as he fell? A couple of teens
with not a trace of a motive said

"Let's hit him"? Or maybe the mob instead
of giving him one more warning leans
hard, so he's found there, shot in the head,

And *he's* the warning: a dose of lead
if you don't pay up is all that it means,
*capisce*? With nothing more to be said.

And that's the item. Carelessly read,
as soon forgotten. Hey, who cares beans?
Some poor stiff turns up shot in the head
in Queens. No suspects, the spokeswoman said.

# HOMO ERECTUS

> We call ourselves wise—*homo sapiens*—and
> argue that our language and art differentiate
> us from other species of animals. We also define
> ourselves by our rising from all fours to a standing
> position, and we call one of our ancestors *homo*
> *erectus*. It has been argued (in the eighteenth
> century by Herder and Humboldt and again more
> recently by physical anthrolopogists) that our
> language ability is directly related to our erect
> posture. We speak because we stand...
>
> — Scott Abbott, from *An Open*
> *World: Essays On Leslie Norris*

We speak because we stand.
Masters because erect.
Posture has made us grand

Lords of the sea and land,
worthy of all respect.
We speak because we stand,

And as we speak, expand
our dominance, elect
ourselves great Pooh-Bahs, grand

Through verbal sleight-of-hand
till all worlds intersect
at any spot we stand,

Mere playthings, to command
and summon and direct.
Oh, what could be as grand

As our enlightened band
that staged this great effect
through boasting how we stand
in language great and grand?

# AN ASTROLOGER AWAITS YOUR CALL

An astrologer awaits your call.
He's waiting right now by the line.
Ask anything. He'll tell you all.

Which stereo should you install?
Will Edna's hearing aid be fine?
An astrologer awaits your call;

Expert, discreet, professional
advice about your life, your sign,
your prospects. He will tell you all

Fate holds in store, what will befall
in sectors human and divine.
An astrologer awaits your call.

Is there a life beyond the Mall?
Will a new love arise and shine?
Just ask, and he'll reveal it all.

Why live entombed? Burst through the wall!
Adults, for just $2.99
(per minute) there awaits your call
an astrologer who'll tell you all!

# FLIP SIDE

> Of course, the flip side of a smile is a wince.
> —David Galef, from a review in *Light*

The flip side of a smile is a wince.
Sometimes the two are really only one.
I learned that young; have practiced ever since

Always at least to seem to smile, for in-
stance, finding saving humor where there's none.
Although the smile is only just a wince,

That casual deception can convince
others to whom spry misery is fun.
I learned that young; I've practiced ever since.

How wily courtiers learn to please a Prince,
the way you treat a madman with a gun:
the flip side of a smile may be a wince,

But knowing few detect a difference,
or care, is how close games are often won.
Learning that young, I've practiced ever since.

So when I smile, kindly ignore the hints
suggesting what in fact is being done.
Unless, of course, you too have learned to wince
and act as if that's just a smile, long since.

# STRANGER

He crouched outside her window where
he'd watched her light switch on before,
and wondered if she would appear,

But also why he shivered there
when he could still approach her door,
be welcomed, talk, then point out where

A man might crouch outside and stare;
a man confused, afraid, unsure...
He wondered if she would appear

Concerned, since, if she seemed to care,
then maybe he could tell her more:
tell why men crouch at windows where

Some woman stands, and don't declare
straight out why they are troubled, or
expect the woman to appear

The least concerned with their despair.
He crouched, determined to ignore
all else except that window where
he hoped, he prayed, she might appear.


## FOR A MOMENT

You were afraid. I was afraid of you,
yet still I asked, and you agreed, to dance;
just for that moment we were more than two

Strangers who ambled in, hung back, and knew
the stakes too high and wild to take a chance.
You were afraid, I was afraid of you,

But somehow something summoned us on cue,
put off our fears, pushed us to touch and glance.
Just for a moment we were more than two,

A moment when we clung and stepped our few
steps, wheeled and whirled our version of romance,
till you grew afraid, I grew afraid of you,

The music petered out. We bowed, withdrew,
nothing remaining but the awkward stance
of ones who had been briefly more than two

Lonely people alone, watching with rue
accomplished couples glide the floor's expanse.
You were afraid, I was afraid of you,
though just for one moment we were more than two.


## THE PATTERN

We made arrangements, but we never met.
The place, the hour were wrong. You had to go;
you sent someone to tell me. I forget

What was so urgent then, except I'd let
myself insist on things I had to know.
We made arrangements, but we never met:

A pattern with you. Any time we'd set
specific hour and place, you'd just not show.
I'd make excuses for you, then forget

Claiming it didn't matter, all regret
wiped out the instant you renewed your glow.
We'd make arrangements, but we never met

And now we never will. Why be upset?
Why spend good time complaining, moaning how
you'd promise you would meet me, then forget,

When I could wager, sure as any bet,
you'd slip away? I even willed it so.
We made arrangements, but we never met?
How often has that happened? I forget.

# CLOSE READING

I scour your words for clues;
some straw that I can clutch.
There isn't any news.

No nuance I can use;
no jot I can detach.
I scour your words for clues

To what we each refuse
to speak about. I watch
for any shred of news,

Hint, minum, glint, or ruse
to build upon or patch
what cannot pass for clues

In vain. Again, I lose,
with not one straw to snatch,
one scintilla of news

To bolster or excuse
this strained excuse for touch.
I scour your words for clues.
There's not one bit of news.


# BETRAYAL

Betrayal is as easy as a word.
A glance, a touch, and what was there is gone.
Sometimes the whisper isn't even heard.

An eye averted, something just inferred
signals the change, though everything goes on
unchecked, unquestioned, easy as a word

Not said, or said in jest, or softly slurred
as if not meant. The hand upon the pawn
hesitates, trembles, wondering what was heard,

Then makes its move. The figures on the board
alter relations slightly; cross the lawn;
align themselves; exchange a casual word

And what was scarcely thought of, deemed absurd,
rejected out-of-hand is now the one
fact in the story everyone has heard

And knows and knew. What cannot be ignored
is trumpeted. What cannot be undone
slips into place as lightly as a word
whispered so softly it was barely heard.


## THIS DANCE

We do this dance, see?
We never come too close.
It keeps us kind of free.

It's simple: one, two, three.
You watch your partner's toes.
We do this dance, see?

You stay away from me.
The air between us flows
and keeps us kind of free

The way we chose to be,
remember, when we chose.
We do this dance, see,

And circle constantly,
whatever comes or goes,
since that's what keeps us free.

Oh, sometimes maybe we
miss out a bit, who knows?
We do this dance, see?
It keeps us kind of free.


## PARTNERS

Nothing much.
Easy access.
Only touch.

Nifty catch;
lucky guess.
Nothing much.

Quick approach.
Little mess:
only touch.

No attach-
ment; no fuss.
Nothing much.

Strike it rich,
more or less,
with a touch,

Till you switch.
Why confess?
What's a touch?
Nothing much.

# FOR THE UNKNOWING HEROES

Let wreaths and medals at your hearts be laid.
Let solemn speeches honor what you lost.
You did not know enough to be afraid.

Tricked out in youthful hopes and dreams, you weighed
as feather-light what sacrifice would cost,
spurning the dirt in which your hearts are laid.

What vows can still be vowed, what prayers be prayed,
by those who have consigned to thankless dust
a gallantry that served them unafraid,

That couldn't conceive the promises they made
concealed sad mockeries of love and trust?
As wreath and medal at your hearts are laid

We mourn in secret how you were betrayed:
high-hearted, selfless, faithful at your post,
you were too ignorant to be afraid,

And entered danger like a sunlit glade,
light glittering off your mail, the fabled just.
May wreaths and medals at your hearts be laid.
You didn't last long enough to be afraid.


# FRAMED, SMILING

We loved a person, and we loved a face.
Now both are somewhere else, not to return,
never to change. A picture takes their place.

Framed, smiling. In a kind of sacred space
it casts its benediction. Candles burn.
We loved a person, and we loved a face

127

Whose features fade. That kiss, that last embrace,
those parting words: all air. We can't discern
such details now. A picture takes their place.

Hurry and loss and time have set the pace
and pipe the tune. We pause, but barely yearn.
We loved a person, and we loved a face,

Oh, loved them past all telling, knew the grace
conferred by love, beyond what love can earn;
touched Paradise. A picture takes their place,

And doesn't. Nothing does. We dust the case,
put back mementos, gradually unlearn
we loved a person, yes, and loved a face
consigned to dust. A picture takes their place.


## THE GARMENT

*The web is woven and you have to wear it.*
— Wallace Stevens

We're down to this at last:
a simple seamless cloak
composed of all our past;

Composed of what was cast
aside, away. A joke.
We're down to this at last.

We thought our choice was vast.
A universe that spoke,
composed of all the Past,

That promised we could mas-
ter all. Nothing but smoke.
We're down to this at last:

Pathetic and harassed,
poor weakly wandering folk,
lost remnants of some past,

Reduced to clinging fast
to one thin thread-bare cloak.
We're down to this at last.
Mere phantoms of our past.


## SOMEHOW

My father could have taught me what he knew.
He would have liked to, but I wasn't ready.
I had to find out for myself what's true.

My teachers would have liked to teach me too.
They hammered out a drumbeat, slow and steady.
But I kept marching to the drum I knew.

I made some friends, a hearty, boisterous crew.
We laughed, and loafed. Their company was heady.
But I set off alone to find what's true.

I lingered on the way. A love or two
cast spells to hold me, but my course held steady.
I would not settle down until I knew.

Somehow I got to here. I muddled through,
true to what truths I learned, however petty.
At least they're mine, and I have found them true.

My son regards the world as if it's new.
I'd like to teach him, but he isn't ready.
Someday he'll wonder what his father knew.
He'll have to find out for himself what's true.

# VALEDICTION

To teach you what you cannot know
requires a lifetime spent in doubt.
Go strong in headstrong youth; but go.

Move on; move out. March past the show
of shadows who by bribe or knout
would teach you what you cannot know,

Would proffer Truth if you bow low
and sing in unison or shout.
Go strong in faith, in hope. But go.

Though you must sing alone, and though
no solitary soul's about
to teach you what you cannot know,

Such dark will grow familiar, grow
stern habit you can't live without.
Go strong in steadfast trust. Yes, go

Until unlooked-for blessings flow
and light that's buried now flares out
to teach you what you cannot know.
Go strong in all our love; but go.


# MOVING TO MUSIC

We take what's given, then we take a chance.
We slowly learn what we will never know.
We grow into the ritual of the dance.

The world yields nothing to the casual glance;
we learn we must go deeper, and we go.
We take what's given, then we take a chance,

Discovering the unaccustomed stance,
accommodating to the heel and toe:
we grow into the ritual of the dance;

Shed easy moves, illusions of romance,
fake lore of progress, luxury of flow.
We take what's given, then we take the chance

That what there is suffices. Nothing fan-
cy; nothing planned. No flourish just for show.
We grow into the ritual of the dance

Until we are the steps, one small expanse
become our only world. We will it so.
We take what's given, then we take a chance.
We grow into the ritual of the dance.


## WHAT MAKES A SONG

You think the play is all, but you are wrong.
There's work involved in getting up the hill.
It takes a steady hand to forge a song,

You learn; to keep it running smooth and strong
commands reserves of energy and will
sufficient to propel it. You are wrong.

Oh, for a while the thing rolls right along.
Then it will stall; then sputter. All falls still.
What does it take, you moan, to make a song,

Glancing around. You're stuck, marooned among
familiar objects, with an unfamil-
iar sense of being lost, where all's gone wrong,

Been botched. But grace flows in, and you belong!
Launched on the tide once more, for good or ill,
no question now that you can forge the song!

So you forge on, and through, until it's sung
and shimmers, graced with play and pluck and skill.
I've got it now, you think, but you are wrong.
You'll never understand what makes a song.

# IV. TAKING OFF

# THE GARDEN

I'm going out to mash a slug or two.
They're wasting my tomatoes, oozing slime
On everything I own.  I think it's time
The bastards learned a lesson.  You come too.


# GARZA

> garza, n.f. Gauze; lint; (Zool.) heron; jaw of a horse.
> —*Cassell's Italian Dictionary*

*Garza* is a funny word
since it can mean a kind of bird

but also lint, and also gauze,
and also, in the plural, jaws

of horses; so, were one to say,
"I'm sad.  My *garza* is away,"

that could mean, "Someone took my bone."
"My heron left me all alone."

"My gauze has slipped."  "I've lost my lint."
The listener would need some hint

and still might not be very sure
of just what to console you for.

A word like *garza* makes one wish
for simple words like "peach" or "dish"

where even when the meaning's double
at least you know why you're in trouble.

# THE FORM

If you fill out your own tax return, you should be able
to understand this form. If you pay someone to fill out
your tax return, you may have difficulty with this form.
— from a letter,
Payroll Office, Harvard University

I don't fill out my own tax return; I am unable to understand
this form.

I pay someone to fill out my tax return; he will be able to
understand this form.

He will have no difficulty with this form; he will carefully
explain it to me.

I still will be unable to understand this form; I will pay him
for explaining it to me.

He will explain it to me again and again; I will continue to pay
him for explaining it.

He will have no difficulty understanding this form; he will
have considerable difficulty explaining it to me.

He will have difficulty understanding why I cannot
understand; I will have difficulty explaining to
him why I cannot understand.

I will also have difficulty paying him, and difficulty explaining
why I am having difficulty paying him.

I will continue to have difficulty understanding why I am
unable to understand.

I will also continue to have difficulty understanding why it
should be necessary that I understand.

Clearly, my difficulties are my own business; they are of no
interest to the people who devise the forms and
send out the letters.

They are of moderate interest to the person who fills out my
tax return, but only so long as I continue to pay him.

# ATTENTION MINIATURE LOVERS

—headline in *The Cricket*, February 1990

Here is the announcement you have been waiting for.
We have succeeded in designing
to the most precise specifications:
tiny sunsets; parks no larger than patios
featuring rolling hills and extensive woodlands;
postage-stamp-sized beds
with canopies and adjustable curtains.

We are also pleased to offer,
for the first time anywhere,
canoes smaller than stickpins
with streams to paddle them on
beneath overarching banks
providing discreet shade and cover.

Yes, it is a world just for you
free from prying eyes
and prurient glances.
And, of course, comes with our guarantee:
you will never be peered at again.

But now for the best part!
After years of research
our technicians have perfected
a means to contract time.
In your world, seconds
will have ceased to exist.
For all practical purposes,
you may henceforth ignore them.

And death?
Well death
continues to pose a challenge

though progress is being made.

Therefore, please watch this space

for subsequent announcements.


### Thomas Wyatt
(1503-1542)

## GOSSIP COLUMNIST'S REVENGE

"They flee from me, that sometime did me seek,"
and laugh behind my back about their games.
Well, two can play at tricks of cheat and sneak.
I've got them down. And I am naming names!


### Christopher Marlowe
(1564-1593)

## THE PASSIONATE BUSINESSMAN TO HIS LOVE

"Come live with me and be my love,"—
Or, better yet, let's meet
Clandestinely, at intervals
Convenient and discreet.


### William Shakespeare
(1564-1616)

## ABRIDGED SONNETS

### 73

"That time of year thou may'st in me behold"
When things are falling off, or getting cold.
My limbs are stiff; there's nothing I can do.
Sweet birds have fled, and now I'm losing you.

"Let me not to the marriage of true minds
Admit impediments." But if I must,
for certain one would have to be the grinds
Of daily life. Another would be lust.


Robert Herrick
(1591-1674)

## P'S AND Q'S

"A sweet disorder in the dress"
is sexier, I must confess,
than when each tiniest detail's right,
fussed over, prissy, prim, and tight!


Andrew Marvell
(1620-1678)

## GIGUNDUS

"My vegetable love should grow
Vaster than empires and more slow;"
Rhubarb, a continent's expanse;
One Brussels sprout, the size of France!


Henry Vaughan
(1622-1695)

## THE EXPERIENCE

"I saw Eternity the other night";
It was so big it gave me quite a fright
Just stretching out as far as I could see.
I got up quick, and turned on the TV.

## Leigh Hunt
(1784-1859)

### TRAVIS LICKED ME

Travis licked me when we met
Leaping from the chaise he'll doze in.
Time, you dog, you love to get
Kisses in your jaws, stick those in.
Say I'm tired, say I'm sad,
Say that men and beasts have tricked me.
Say I smell like bones, but add
Travis licked me.


## Samuel Taylor Coleridge
(1772-1834)

### VIRTUOSO PERFORMANCE

"In Xanadu did Kubla Khan"
a mighty splendid show put on.
Those caves of ice! That dome in air!
But only Coleridge was there.


## William Wordsworth
(1770-1850)

### STRANGE CORRESPONDENCE

Strange correspondence have we had,
Yet he would be a liar
Who claimed to read a single word
I now commit to fire.

So, Lucy, do the same with mine:
Let all go up in smoke!
They'll call us lovers, doomed, divine...
(And we can share the joke.)

## KO'D

"A slumber did my spirit seal;"
in fact, it knocked me out!
I was a zombie all day long
and barely got about.

So now I've taken to my bed;
I lie here, stiff and white,
in terror lest it come again
and knock me out tonight!

## THE MOMENT OF FRIVOLITY

"Surprized by joy—" A gust removed my hat.
I stopped; suppressed a smile.  Enough of that!

## Percy Bysshe Shelley
(1792-1822)

## UPSTATE

"If Winter comes, can Spring be far behind?"
Where I live, yes; long months, so grim and glum
The snow lies blanker than a poet's mind
Who'd say a thing so pitiful and dumb.

Emily Dickinson
(1830-1886)

## FROM THE WORKPLACE

"Tell all the Truth but tell it slant—"
Be careful what you say—
They're going to call you on the Rug—
They're going to make you pay—

They'll have your Head—they'll have your Hide—
They'll hang it on the Wall—
Say nothing that you can't deny—
Or claim—you can't—recall


Robert Browning
(1812-1889)

## MEMORABILIA

Ah, did I once see Shelley plain,
    And did she make a little face
And tell me not to look again
    Or I must leave her place?

And did I blush, but still make sure
    I got a full view of each breast
Till I got booted out the door?
    Well, I forget the rest!


William Ernest Henley
(1849-1903)

## INVICTUS?

Your head is bloody, but unbowed? If so,
don't boast, lest it receive another blow.

Henry Wadsworth Longfellow
(1807-1882)

## CUPID'S QUIVER

I shot my seed into the air
It landed here, it landed there
I know it's not the thing to do
But, Valentine, I thought of you


Oscar Wilde
(1856-1900)

## THE DANGEROUS CLIFFS

You always kill the thing you love.
So runs the curse.  A
fellow gives his gal a shove
or vice versa.


Emma Lazarus
(1849-1887)

## THE LADY SPEAKS AGAIN

"I lift my lamp beside the golden door."
More golden now than ever; don't ask why.
Just list your assets, where you can get more,
and who you know. No others need apply.

A. E. Housman
(1859-1936)

# EPITAPH ON A DISGRUNTLED ACADEMIC

You, on the days when Heaven was falling,
  When any schism raised its head,
Stood steadfast in your sacred calling
  And fought pitched battles and are dead.

Your shoulders held the sky suspended;
  Your tantrums kept all change at bay;
What deans abandoned, you defended,
  And made all others rue the day.

Rudyard Kipling
(1865-1936)

# A LIVE POLITICIAN

"I could not dig: I dared not rob:
Therefore I lied to please the mob."
I stole in office; used my place
To help my nephew in disgrace.
Got caught; got censured; spoke, with tears.
And now I'm back for six more years.

Wallace Stevens
(1879-1955)

# TEN OR SO WAYS OF LOOKING AT THE PIGEONS

I

In the whole piazza
the only bulging thing
is the purse of the pigeon-man.

## II

They bob and waddle and strut.
They perch on your hand and your head.
They shit on your shirt.

## III

I was of no mind,
like a piazza full of pigeons
when there aren't any people.

## IV

A child and a pigeon
are two.
A child and a pigeon and corn
are a seething mass
of pigeons.

## V

O stout man from McAllen,
why don't you watch where you're going?
You almost trampled a pigeon.

## VI

At the sight of scrawny necks
and sooty feathers
even an ornithologist
would cry out in revulsion!

## VII

The pigeons' eyes are dull.
The tourists must be flying.

## VIII

I do not know which to prefer,
pigeons that are dead
or those that are merely absent.

## IX

I rode through Florence
in a crummy coach.
Once I had a hope
we'd stop at a spot
not yet encrusted by pigeons

## X

It was noisy all day.
It will be noisy tonight.
And tomorrow, smack, at dawn—
the goddam cooing of pigeons.


William Butler Yeats
(1865-1939)

## MTV

"How can we know the dancer from the dance?"
Turn off the sound, and then you stand a chance.


## THE MORSEL

*Crumpets should always be served warm...*
— Cuthbert Giles

How can I, that crumpet there
Nestled in its steam,

Care how cities fall apart
While politicians scheme?
Around the bar the old farts rant
On AIDS and drugs and crime,
And here's a younger fart who swears
He just won't vote next time,
And maybe what they claim is true
Of chaos north and south,
But O that I had teeth again
And held it in my mouth!


## ALTERNATIVE ADVICE TO A FRIEND
## WHOSE WORK HAS COME TO NOTHING

"Be secret and take defeat"?
Crawl off somewhere and cry,
letting them taste the sweet
revenge of knowing why
you're acting so discreet?
No! Fasten them with your eye.
Hint you will make them sweat
with what you've learned. Imply
those they most hate and fear
are poised to smash them. Lie.
Act like the trap's been set.
Torture them with the bait.
Keep your ears open. Wait.
Then blow them all sky-high!


## LOST TIME

"You think it horrible that lust and rage
Should dance attendance upon my old age"?
I never kissed a girl till I was thirty,
And thought that even holding hands was dirty!

Ezra Pound
(1885-1972)

A VISITATION

"Thank you, whatever comes." And then she split.
Ye Gods! We talk of Beauty. That was it!

T. S. ELIOT
(1888-1965)

DISCOURS ENERVANT

In the rooms the women doze or slumber
impervious to *ennui*. They have our number.

William Carlos Williams
(1883-1963)

THE DOCTOR DRIVES TO WORK

(discarded version)

At ten A.M. the young housewife
moves about in negligee behind
the wooden walls of her husband's house.
I drive round and round the block.

But now she comes to the curb
to call the ice-man, fish-man, and stands
shy, uncorseted, tucking in
stray ends of hair. She's more beautiful even
than I remembered her!

My hand dives into my lap
as I creep by and leer at her
through the steamed-up windows of my car.


## AGED WHACHAMACALLIT

I must tell you

this thingamajig
with its whatsis
extended

out
past even
wherever

it stuck
before
when I showed you

before remember
or did

I just tell you


Robert Frost
(1874-1963)

## A DOG'S LIFE

The old poet growls without getting up.
No one remembers when he was a pup.

## E.P.A.

We dance round in a ring and propose
while the problem squats at the center and glows.


## STORM WARNING

"She is as in a field a silken tent"
which, when a gust comes, flaps and snaps, then slips
free of all ties, drops in a heap, or rips
skyward, and leaves us wondering where it went.


## W. H. Auden
(1907-1973)

## READERS' RIGHTS

> *Some poems which I wrote and, unfortunately,
> published, I have thrown out because they were
> dishonest, or bad-mannered, or boring.*

Auden, with this lame excuse,
Changed his poems to fit his views;
Left us searching for the verse
He omitted, or made worse;

Left us wishing he'd let stand
Works of youthful heart and hand.
Readers have the right to quarrel
When their bard has grown too moral.

# INCIDENT AT THE GATE

A poet of avowed ambition
applies discreetly for admission.
A Presence gathers in the gloom.
"Begone!" growls Guardian Harold Bloom.

"I only want a small position
within the manifold Tradition."
"I'm sorry, but there isn't Room,"
propounds Custodian Harold Bloom.

"But here's a *bona fide* petition!
You can't withhold your recognition..."
"That's something one should not presume,"
pontificates the Pontiff Bloom.

"The Devil take your Sacred Mission!
Go cram your stuffy Exhibition!"
"We now consign you to your Doom,"
intones Pantocrator Harold Bloom.


# W. S. MERWIN MEDITATES ON A CLOUD

Everything is always
passing it never
passes it is always
about to pass like that white
bird see it is
moving it is not
moving it is barely
moving it is not
even a bird it's
a ship no it's
a nun

151

# CHARLES SIMIC FINDS HIMSELF NOWHERE, EVERYWHERE ALL AT ONCE

In a street full of forever
I wander past nameless nothings
Wishing I were somewhere else.
In some other poem, for instance.


# DAVID IGNATOW EXAMINES HIS MOTIVES

Because I am honest
I beat people
with the club of my honesty
expecting them in turn
to beat me
which they do unmercifully
because why else
were we handed these clubs
each one brandishing a club
unless it is to beat oneself
which I also do
needing intervals of refreshment


# THE POET REDGROVE

*Redgrove is one of the very few contemporary poets
who actually blazes at his readers...*

—a blurb

Quick! Hit the dirt! Take cover! Down!
The poet Redgrove's back in town

With weapons fiercer far than Byron's.
No man dare stand in his environs.

He's mad! He's mean! He's out to get you!
The undertaker's bound to fetch you

If you attempt to sneak one look.
For God's sake, reader! Drop that book!

# MARY OLIVER ELECTS TO LEAVE HER KITCHEN

I am not saying
that's not food
on my table,

and if I ate it
it wouldn't become me.
It is,

and it would.
No,
I am not saying that.

Nor am I saying
it wouldn't be good
if I did,

since I will
because I must.
No, I am not saying that either.

All I am saying
is right now
I am just not hungry enough,

so I will tramp
into the swamp
where the animals eat one another,

and are eaten in turn,
and turn into each other,
and then into the swamp,

and I will watch,
and I will watch myself
as I am watching,

and that
should give me an appetite.

## A BUDDY OF HOUSMAN'S

"Why must you be always thinking,
Lad? The world's a place for drinking,
Warring, whoring. What the hell?
Write it down, and you'll do well."

## GRADUATE "ASSISTANT"

"Did she put on his knowledge with his power
before the indifferent beak could let her drop?"

## THE HANDSOME POET

The handsome poet
doesn't need to write poems
that are poems,
or even poems
that other people think
are poems.

Why should he?

He is the handsome poet.

He writes about being
himself.

*

The handsome poet
writes about being handsome

because that is what other people
want him to write about

and he writes about being a poet

because that is also what other people
want him to write about

and he writes about being the handsome poet

because that is especially what other people
want him to write about.

Sometimes, he concludes, it's a bore
being only the handsome poet

and he writes about that.

*

People shower gifts
on the handsome poet.

Honors.

Awards.

Girls throw themselves at his feet
and elsewhere.

Ladies invite him to tea
and more.

Young men cart along books
for him to sign.

"What's your secret?" they ask.

He smiles,
more handsome than ever.

"I have no secret,"
he replies.

*

The handsome poet
wonders how it would be
to be not so handsome.

He looks at poems.

Studies them.

Puzzles over them.

He crinkles his handsome nose.

*Hard,* he thinks

*How hard it would be,* he thinks

*to be just a poet.*


## DEAR WRITER

In reply to your recent inquiry,
we have lost your poems.

If we had not,
we would undoubtedly have said unkind things;
therefore we consider
we have done you a favor.

Should you have others,
we wish you better luck
in placing them elsewhere.

Sincerely, The Editors

P.S. Enclosed please find the revised guidelines
for renewing your subscription.

## THE REVIEWER

The reviewer
tells you a great deal
about himself.

That way
you can understand
why he understands.

*

You must not
antagonize
the reviewer.

That will only
make him angry.

You must not
seek to placate
the reviewer.

That will also
make him angry.

*

Do not expect
mercy
from the reviewer.

That is not his business.

His business
is to dispense
precise justice.

Why else
has he become
the reviewer?

*

At night the reviewer
removes his clothes.

Lies down alone.

Lets himself go.

In his dreams
he could be anyone

even those
he reviews.

He revels
in their inadmissable
license.


## PERFORMANCE

You know the steps, the gestures, and the glance.
The music starts, and now you have your chance.
You do your imitation of a dance.

# THE MINOR MINOR POETS

In quatrains trim we mourn our fate
And frame our desolation.
The train we boarded wasn't late;
It never left the station!


# FAMOUS POET UNABLE TO APPEAR,
# AUDIENCE FAILS TO SHOW UP

A tape recorder
reads to a tape recorder.


# MACK THE EPIGRAM

So deft his thrust, so lightning-swift and true,
his victim stammered "Thanks!" before he knew.


# ON BEING INSTRUCTED TO SEND ON A CHAIN LETTER

A chance to have *five* readers? Friendly too?
The chain be hanged! I send this poem to you.

# EMILY DICKINSON'S WRITING GROUP

The procedure took a while to establish.
Eventually, it was this: she would slip
a few poems, in a sealed envelope,
under a door; wait a prescribed time;
then retrieve the envelope. There were
to be no comments. It was understood
that each poem was to be examined
in precisely the spirit in which
it was written, and in an attitude of
reverence, affection, and total attention.

Emily credited her achievement to membership
in this group, which, among its benefits,
relieved her of the obligation to publish
and be recognized. In one of her lost letters,
she refers to it as "Utterly Congenial
and Gratifying." In another, she extols it
as offering "Unquestionably—the Best Criticism—
I shall hope to Receive—"

# V. FLYING HIGH: NEW POEMS

# AN AMERICAN LANDSCAPE

The couples in the golfcarts are identical,
white-haired mannikins returning to dwellings

So similar those who inhabit them
can barely tell them apart

Along roads that wind and wind only to arrive
at others indistinguishable from them

Lined also with lawns trimmed to resemble
billiard tables, which sport vegetation

Coifed and teased as if to bewilder
the outsider who by now imagines himself

Bewitched, capable of observing
only the variants of a single bush,

One lone tree, that cactus standing sentinel
above the same rock, on which there crouches

A single
plastic

gecko.


# THE EQUIVALENT OF SIBERIA

"Welcome to my world,"
he mumbles,

shovel
futile against the glut
of the clogged
compactor.

"Worst job in the college.
I told them—"

He stops.

His anger exudes
a palpable stench.

"No one around here—"
he gives the stinking mound
a ferocious jab—

"can do anything right."

*

He lost his job in the mailroom
(rumor has it)
because of "attitude."

No one will comment
officially.

Unofficially
(rumor also has it)
he dipped into
petty cash.

Student workers claim
he was "railroaded."

"If something can be done wrong
in this goddam place,"
he hisses

"that's how they'll do it."

*

The compactor grinds,
whirs,
as he flips
and flips the switch.

The pile shudders,
heaves,
but goes
nowhere.

He flings the shovel,
grabs a pole,
steadies himself

then attacks it
again and again.

## THE DEVIL AND REVEREND SMOOTHTONGUE

"The Devil can quote Scripture."
So Reverend Smoothtongue said.
"But I can quote the Devil
and turn him on his head."

The Devil came to Smoothtongue.
"I hear you're quite the man."
Smoothtongue smiled at the Devil.
"I do the best I can."

The Devil looked him over.
"I'd say you fit the bill.
Come serve as my Lieutenant.
I've got a house to fill."

Then Smoothtongue looked at the Devil.
"You know I serve the Lord.
That train is bound for glory.
Why don't you hop aboard?"

"I'll tell you," said the Devil.
"That train will jump the track.
Those souls on board are my souls,
and they ain't comin' back."

The Devil and Reverend Smoothtongue,
they argued through the night.
They argued and they argued
until the morning light.

They argued and they argued,
and neither would give in.
The Devil and Reverend Smoothtongue
debated points of sin.

"My boy, now I believe you.
You sure can make a case,"
the Devil said to Smoothtongue.
"You're welcome to my place.

Come down for some refreshments.
I think they'll suit you fine.
There's flocks of fancy women
and vats of rare old wine.

There's cash for just the askin'
to use just how you please.
That church you'd die or kill for?
It's yours, without the fees."

Well, no one knows for certain
but there are some who say
the Devil and Reverend Smoothtongue
been buddies since that day.

No, no one ever caught them,
but there are those who swear
that when the Rev quotes Scripture
there's sulphur in the air.


## IN CONFIDENCE

"Am I going to get in trouble if
I talk to you?"

He peers around.

"Of course not."

I push the button. The machine
starts to whir.

"Because there are a lot of people - "

"You'll be fine. I promise. Go ahead."

He hesitates, then begins. The words
spill out.

Already, I can see and hear it. Outrage.
Recriminations. The poor guy will be
hounded, and slaughtered like an animal.

They'll have his guts hanging
on a line.

The poor sap. You'd think he'd have
learned something by now. Just one
little thing.

Where do they get these guys?

# THE KINDNESS OF STRANGERS

"You've a mighty fine house," said a crafty old fox,
who had slipped through the wires and picked all the locks.

"I'm a buddy, you know, of old Waldo, the hound.
Poor old thing, he's exhausted, and can't hear a sound.

And your boss, Farmer Bob, well, he's tucked in real tight.
No, a five-alarm fire wouldn't rouse him tonight.

So I guess it's just us. It's a shame and a crime
that there's no one to help you and no end of time.

Oh, I pity poor chickens, but what can one do?
It's a pretty rum world, and the options are few.

You can sit there and cluck. You can flap. You can flail.
There's a chance you'll survive, but it's likely you'll fail.

And it isn't your fault. Heaven knows, you've done well.
Why, you've been the best chickens you could since your shell.

You've been honest and upright and courteous and kind.
You deserve to be happy. My friends, Fate is blind.

I just act as its agent. I know this is crap.
It could happen to me. I'll get caught in a trap

Or get shot or get poisoned, just doing my job.
And the same's true for Waldo. The same's true for Bob.

It's a mess, and me yakking won't sort the thing out.
A conundrum for certain, and chock-full of doubt.

It would take someone wiser and deeper by far
to give counsel and comfort about how things are;

To give counsel and comfort and make them okay,
what a boon that would be! What a glorious day!

If we all understood! Wing and paw, fur and feather,
we could join in a dance. We could lie down together.

But enough of palaver and straining of wits.
You'll forgive me. I need to get back to my kits."


*To be told just how bad things are isn't much fun*
*when the fat's in the fire, the slug's in the gun.*


### Wolves advance to semis

— sports headline

We didn't notice 'em at first, intent as we were
on gettin' into the circle: mud; a broken axle
on Rafe's 18-wheeler; that first attack near Munsville
where we nearly lost Higgins. We were too busy
haulin' in branches, gettin' the fires up and blazing.

Then that kid strayed off, one of Amy's little ones;
she started screamin', Rudy sounded the alarm,
everyone runnin' everywhichway hollerin'
till they found him huddled in somebody's cab.
I guess we thought we were home free.

Sure, sure, I know,
we let our guard down. We knew better, oughta of, anyway,
'specially after Latham Valley Road. I suppose
we were just plain exhausted.

So Carl's handin' out rifles when he stops dead;
motions everyone to be still.

We couldn't hear 'em but we could sense 'em
sure as anything. They were out there; it was like
you could feel shadows moving. Some kid whimpers
and gets shut up quick. Little sounds from the edge of the woods
and comin' up from the creekbed. Could'a been any night sounds,
if you didn't know better.

We knew better.

LeBray flicks on his torchlamp, shines it out
under one of the hitches, swings it in an arc.

Holds it a moment, then lets out a whistle.

Lights 'em up.


## THE SKEPTICAL PRINCE

He thinks he caught a glimpse once; heard a song.
But that was long ago. He could be wrong.
He'd scale the tower, burst the bonds, he'll swear,
if she'll just give some token she is there.

The town has grown accustomed to the sight:
he drinks by day, then hangs around at night,
purveying sad and antiquated lore,
insisting he will act once he is sure.

His horse is stabled elsewhere. He'll decide,
he claims, the day, the hour, he will ride.
He's waiting for a sign. He wants it known
his purpose holds. And he'll not leave alone.

# CENTRIFUGAL

She leaves him with their children; cannot stay
to watch her life bleed silently away
in daily hassle, heartache, thankless chore;
harsh duties she'd been taught her life was for.

He thinks: *If I had known, if I had known....*
Clenches a fist. *I can't do this alone,*
*God damn her!* He would love to smash her face,
and wonders who he'll find to take her place.

They blame their mother, blame their father too.
They want her back. They don't know what to do.
They blame themselves. Each night, upon their knees,
they bargain with their Heavenly Father: *Please....*

# DYING GENERATIONS

The old professors hobble and shuffle and dote,
benign now, quiet, their gossip a muted chirr
of long-past passion and change, debate and vote;
the time they inhabit now: the times that were.

Meanwhile, grandchildren frolic. Some play croquet,
some horseshoes; a flock are sprawled out on the lawn,
bored with the bustle, the food, the talk, the day,
impatient for hot-breathed dark, with all of this gone.

# CREATURE ENVY

That waterbug, whose life is spent
gliding a shifting element,
is neither uptight nor intent;

He simply skates, now fast, now slow,
not conscious that he does not know
vicissitude of ebb and flow;

Blithe, graceful, wholly unaware
what swoops or hovers in the air
or lurks around, beneath him there.

Insouciance one might exchange
for constant consciousness of dan-
ger, amplitude of scope and range.


## SAVING A MITE

I puff you off before I turn the page,
a vast expanse more perilous than it looks.
You would have perished, neither sane nor sage,
and not the first to be done in by books.


## EXEMPLUM

I have observed the patient toiling ant.
I have not heard her say, "I won't. I can't."
She hefts incessantly what's twice her size.
A worker, yes. But who would call her wise?


## AMBITION

The moth that flits, again and yet again,
against the brilliant surface of the light,
not knowing what or how or where or when,
guided by neither intellect nor sight,
is no fit emblem for the quest of men
who often blind themselves through being bright.

# HOMUNCULUS LOST AND FOUND

## HOMUNCULUS FURIOSO

"You'll all be sorry!" (*fists clenched*) "Just you wait!"
Homunculus reviews his sorry state;
reviles his fellows, taller and secure.
"Hush, little man. We've heard it all before."

*

## BRAVE BEGINNING

Homunculus recalls: he wasn't small.
Why, no one ever mentioned size at all.
Everything fit, and he was quite the man.
He strode and strutted, shouting out: "I can!"

*

## REFLECTING AND REFLECTIVE

The world at large is hostile and remote.
He has no friends, no clout, no voice, no vote.
Closer to home, the mirror meets his glare.
*A sorry sight,* he thinks. *There's nothing there.*

*

## DAY LABOR

Homunculus sets out to serve; is met
by "Sorry"; "Move along now"; "We regret...."
until he wonders: "What have I to give?"
He quips: "They also serve who merely live?"

## HOMUNCULUS INDULGES IN FANTASIES OF VIOLENCE

The Big Boys play and win; they cheat and steal.
There isn't any way to cut a deal
when no one knows you're there or lets you in.
He'd like to kill them. *Let the games begin!*

\*

## HOMUNCULUS RESOLVES TO CULTIVATE HIS GARDEN

He'd like to kill them? Dazed, he looks around.
What's his complaint? He's got a plot of ground,
two hands, a back (however weak), some seed.
*If no one takes it, what else do I need?*

\*

## AND ACHIEVES A SORT OF SALVATION

The Great World grinds along. At times, at peace,
Homunculus can make its clamor cease.
The little world he mastered keeps him whole
enough: a tiny being with a soul.

\*

## HOMUNCULUS ANSWERS THE QUESTION, *IS LIFE WORTH THE CANDLE?*

Whatever is, just is. It isn't right,
God knows (or doesn't). Still, a little light
can point the way, at least, and help him guess.
So he's still game? Homunculus says yes.

# BURYING PETS

*The fact is people bury people because they have to,*
*they bury pets because they want to.*
— Pet Haven Cemetery & Crematory
For Those Who Care

We had to bury Cal and Uncle Lou,
Aunt Hetty, Sally, Clyde, and Granpa Ned;
we buried Fluffy because we wanted to.

It's not that there was nothin' else to do.
She woulda looked real pretty in the shed.
We had to bury them and Uncle Lou,

You know, or else the neighbors would go "Phew!"
and snoop, the way folks do when someone's dead.
We buried Fluff because we wanted to,

Though Jarvis joked, "Let's make her into stew."
I swear, that boy! I knocked him on the head.
He's going to turn out just like Uncle Lou!

Fluffy was somethin' else. So sweet and true;
I loved it when she butted me in bed.
I'll miss her fierce. That's why I wanted to

Keep her around, like, stuff her. All made new.
But Pa was right. We buried her instead.
She's got a headstone, just like Uncle Lou.
We buried Fluffy because we wanted to.

# COMMON PROPERTY

the song was Rome, the art was Roman still:
the syllables kept order in their pain.
— from To Ovid, From Army Barracks,
Oscar Mandel

"the syllables kept order in their pain."
Now there's a line so good who would not steal,
or borrow? See, I give it back again.

And that's what poets do. They don't explain;
they don't apologize. It's no big deal.
"the syllables kept order in their pain"

Is offered free. Its author doesn't gain
or lose. It's there for all to learn and feel.
It's ours and his. We give it back again

To others, who in turn, as in a chain,
will pass it on. It's good because it's real.
It orders as it teaches us that pain

Can be controlled and useful; can sustain
us even, and through artistry reveal
that what we lose and suffer comes again

As something we can love that will remain
inviolable, a mantra that can heal.
"the syllables kept order in their pain"
is ours now to repeat, again, again.

# HOW TO WRITE A VILLANELLE

You find a line that sounds good. It might do.
But one is not enough. You have to try
to come up with another. It takes two

That bear repeating, that can get you through,
that let you know the thing is going to fly.
First find one line that sounds good, that will do,

Then pair it with a partner. Just a few
rhymes are required. Stringent rules apply,
but you're on top of things once you have two

Lines that go well together, though it's true
you need to find one more to satisfy
the form's demands: a *b* rhyme. When you do

(remembering that all *b* rhymes are new,
and that the whole must flow as well as tie
neatly together, weaving in the two

Lines that repeat, yet change as you review
what's come before, what's still to come)—but why
complicate matters? All you've got to do
is find one line to start with. Make that two.

# REINED IN

The problem of the sonnet, as I see it,
is, you must move in lock step with the form.
However footloose you might like to be, it
creeps back, tail tucked, ears flattened, to the norm.
You sense it all beforehand; know its turnings,
the way it's going to soothe you with a rhyme;
a steady, safe account, with solid earnings,
performance you can bank on anytime,
but wouldn't you like to sometime hit a homer?
Surprise yourself? Go bonkers, haywire, ape?
Astonish others? Shatter that misnomer
they know you as? Find life a different shape?
You're hot to chuck it all? Break out? Burst free?
The cozy sonnet's not your cup of tea.